Shakespeare without a Life

Oxford Wells Shakespeare Lectures

Shakespeare without a Life

MARGRETA DE GRAZIA

OXFORD
UNIVERSITY PRESS

Great Clarendon Street, Oxford, OX2 6DP,
United Kingdom

Oxford University Press is a department of the University of Oxford.
It furthers the University's objective of excellence in research, scholarship,
and education by publishing worldwide. Oxford is a registered trade mark of
Oxford University Press in the UK and in certain other countries

Published in the United States of America by Oxford University Press
198 Madison Avenue, New York, NY 10016, United States of America

British Library Cataloguing in Publication Data

Data available

Library of Congress Control Number: 2022945723

ISBN 978–0–19–881254–8

DOI: 10.1093/oso/9780198812548.001.0001

Printed by Integrated Books International, United States of America

To Colin Thubron, more than ever

Contents

List of Figures

Introduction

For a good two centuries after his death, Shakespeare had no biography. The makings of one were not available. No chronology had been devised by which to integrate the events of his life with the writing of his works. Nor was there an archive of primary materials on which to base a Life. In addition, the only work by Shakespeare written in the first person, the Sonnets, had yet to be critically edited and incorporated into his canon. Before 1800, the biography deemed essential to our understanding and appreciation of Shakespeare simply did not exist. This book is about Shakespeare's survival for those first many generations without one.

How could there ever have been a time when Shakespeare had no Life? Surely after the publication of the grand folio of *Mr. William Shakespeares Comedies, Histories, & Tragedies* (1623) readers would have wanted to know about the man who wrote those thirty-six plays. How else to do so but by finding out about his life? The seventeenth-century notices about him that circulated may be disappointingly scant, recording little more, for example, than that Shakespeare was born in Stratford, wrote plays, and was buried in the town of his nativity. All the same, are they not the first stirrings of the biographical impulse? In the eighteenth century, Nicholas Rowe prefaces his 1709 edition of Shakespeare with a forty-page essay modestly titled *Some Account of the Life, &c. of Mr. William Shakespear* and it is reproduced throughout the eighteenth century. This, too, advances the biographical project. Not only does this account increase the store of what Rowe terms "Personal Stor[ies]," it also for the first time consults an official document, the Stratford parish register. Shouldn't these early efforts be viewed as steps, however small and faltering, in the direction of what we now have: a standard narrative of Shakespeare's life, based on documents and drawing on his works?

Indeed that is how the history of Shakespeare's biography has been told, and insuperably, by Samuel Schoenbaum. His *Shakespeare's Lives*, first published in 1970, has been superseded only by his own revised edition twenty years later. It covers the same two centuries that are my focus here, but throughout it assumes what I question: the existence from the start of the biographical impulse, what he terms "the quest for knowledge of Shakespeare the man." In his comprehensive account, the fragmentary notices and anecdotal clusters of the seventeenth and eighteenth centuries are all advancing toward that knowledge. The quest takes a "quantum leap" forward with the work of the editor and biographer Edmond Malone whose contribution to Shakespeare's biography, according to Schoenbaum, is unrivaled: "Malone found out more about Shakespeare than anyone before or since." His findings fill up the 500-pages of Malone's "masterly *Life of Shakspeare*," intended as the first volume of his posthumously published edition, *The Plays and Poems of William Shakspeare* (1821). At long last, a proper biography had arrived to preface the works. Its arrival, for Schoenbaum, was none too soon: "[H]ow desperately needed that biography was!"[1]

Shakespeare without a Life exempts the first two centuries after Shakespeare's death from that desperate need. Nothing resembling a biography appears at the forefront of Shakespeare's 1623 folio, reproduced three times during the seventeenth century. Instead of a Life, elegiac notices of Shakespeare's death precede the plays. Only the date of his death is given, as if it were the only one of import. Emphatically posthumous, the massive folio volume presents itself as a monument, a bibliographic *tome* that serves as a monumental *tomb* preserving the deceased poet's literary remains. So prefaced, the plays appear to have emerged not from Shakespeare's life but in consequence of his death. Even the Droeshout engraving on the title page seems oddly inanimate, less a portait, perhaps, than an open-eyed death mask.

Two centuries after the 1623 Folio, an edition of Shakespeare's plays and poems was published that places an extensive Life at its forefront. The edition orders the plays chronologically, according to the dates when Shakespeare, by the editor's reckoning, had written them. Not only the biography but the entire edition is stocked with documents, in appendices, addenda, and annotations, all relating however tangentially to Shakespeare. It also includes the 1609 *Sonnets* in an apparatus that links them to Shakespeare's life.[2] This is the posthumous 1821 edition of Malone, the scholar credited with having uniquely advanced the quest for biographical knowledge. But by my account, no such quest was yet underway for him to advance. Not only is there no continuity between the earlier accounts and Malone's biography: the two are mutually exclusive. Indeed the beginnings of Malone's biography can be seen in his copious annotations to Rowe's *Some Account of the Life* in Malone's first edition of Shakespeare (1790) where he systematically refutes virtually every incident Rowe relates.[3] The facts, dates, and documents he has deployed to invalidate Rowe's reports in 1790 form the basis of the *Life of Shakspeare* that he prefixes to his edition of 1821.[4]

My challenge in this book is twofold: first, to propose that what we understand by biography was neither desired nor attempted until late into the eighteenth century; second, to demonstrate that by looking for faint intimations of what is now the norm, we efface the very different priorities once at work. Each of my four chapters focuses on the early absence of what is now indispensable: a biographical narrative, a chronology for the life and the works, an archive or primary materials, and a canon with the 1609 *Sonnets* at its heart. My end throughout is to bring into view what the later fixation on biography has effectively phased out.

My first chapter, "Shakespeare without a Life (1564–1616)," explains what I mean by a "Life" by referencing the biographical formula made standard by the *Dictionary of National Biography* (1885–1900): two dates conjoined by an en dash and enclosed in parentheses: "Shakespeare, William (1564–1616)." (The two dates symbolize the endpoints of the life, the long dash the linear narrative connecting them, and the brackets the free-standing autonomy of the unit.) In the case of Shakespeare, none of these requirements can be met until long after his death: the birthdate is late to be fixed, the chronological continuum even later to be ascertained, and a coherent linear narrative not attempted until Malone. Shakespeare is known instead through a scattering of undated episodic incidents. Yet these anecdotes or "traditional stories" give a strong impression of Shakespeare. Repeatedly they catch him in an act of transgression, breaking the laws of the land or overstepping the bounds of civility. While no support for such offensive behavior can be found in the historical record, confirmation exists elsewhere: in early criticism of Shakespeare's style. Invariably in this early period, his plays are criticized as "irregular" or "unruly," the result of his rustic education that left him short of the mastery of the Greek and Roman models and tongues expected of a poet. The waywardness ascribed to his life is in keeping with the signature "extravagance" of his works—until the next century, when the latter was revalorized as originality and genius and its author assigned an appropriately respectable character.

Chapter 2, "Shakespeare's Lifeline," focuses on the eighteenth-century novelty of the chronological timeline. As events in Shakespeare's life could be dated by documents and situated on a continuum, so, too, could his plays, once the dates of their composition could be plausibly ascertained. When reduced to the common denominator of dates, the plays could be fitted into the progressing trajectory of his lifetime. Before the plays were chronologized, the presiding category had been the ancient one of genre, as foregrounded in both the title and the organization of the 1623 Folio. That Shakespeare's plays seemed to flout the genres, that histories had no classical precedent, only made for more challenging critical debate. Eighteenth-century editions introduce refinements to the Folio's tripartite division, but never with regard to where the plays belonged in Shakespeare's life. The tragedies, for example, are subdivided according to the genre of their source, so that "Tragedies from History" are differentiated from "Tragedies from Fable." When chronological order is observed, in the tragedies as with the histories, it is that of a play's setting in world history rather than that of the two decades in which Shakespeare is thought to have written his plays.

As the chronological structure for a biographical narrative was lacking, so, too, were the primary materials. Chapter 3, "Shakespeare's Archive," concerns the exhaustive search at the end of the eighteenth century for materials in Shakespeare's own hand: for autograph manuscripts, correspondence, even Shakespeare's pocket notebook. Intervening generations are castigated for their failure to preserve and transmit what even scholars imagine as a physical repository of some kind. And yet the fantasized chest never surfaces—indeed it most likely never had existed—except through the initially acclaimed forgeries of William-Henry Ireland. All that could be recovered in Shakespeare's hand were several variable signatures and assorted documents in the hands of his contemporaries, the latter at one remove, as it were, from his own hand. But earlier modes of record-keeping existed, that neither prioritized primary materials nor mistrusted mediation, as can be seen in Gerard Langbaine's alphabetized inventory of plays, *An Account of the English Dramatick Poets* (1691) and John Aubrey's quirky manuscript collection of lives, now known as *Brief Lives* (c. 1676–92).

The final chapter, "The 'deceasèd I' of the 1609 *Sonnets*," concerns the absence of the work that became the most closely affiliated with Shakespeare's biography. It is also the only work by Shakespeare that expressly aspires to everlasting life, ironically as it turns out, for it came close to extinction. The "eternal lines" of the 1609 *Sonnets* were out of print for a century and not fully incorporated into the canon until almost a century after that. For most of that long stretch, the sonnets were ensconced in an eclectic miscellany published in 1640, *Poems: Written by Wil. Shakespeare*. Though deemed spurious and worthless by 1800, the sonnets in the 1640 format endured longer than they had in the authentic 1609 quarto. What gave the sonnets in their 1640 makeover their power to endure? Certainly it was not the promise of access to the life of the poet. Through its distancing and generalizing rubrics, the 1640 miscellany rendered the sonnets quite impersonal. How then did the 1640 *Poems* secure, at least for a time, a future for them? How did they capture what the Sonnets presume for themselves: the literary attention of ages yet unborn? And might the Sonnets themselves, with their many gestures of self-cancellation, have imagined their own survival without "the hand that writ them"?

All four chapters are intended to draw attention to what is lost when the past is imagined as anticipatory of the present. Biography, according to such an expectation, was always in the process of coming into being. The attraction of such an approach is obvious. Once it has a telos, in this case a biography of Shakespeare that follows the programmatic (1564–1616) outline, the approach casts its starting point as far back as possible, here to the earliest notices about Shakespeare, and extends its trajectory forward toward its present familiar use. This construal of the past looks wonderfully comprehensive; everything between then and now takes the form first of incipient and then of developing versions of the present. The past is thereby not only ostensibly preserved but also made relevant. There is, however, a strict bias to this apparent inclusivity. For the trajectory carries forward only what can be construed in its own contemporary image. What resists it, falls by the wayside.

Shakespeare without a Life proceeds another way. It looks not for earlier indications of present imperatives but for what those imperatives have occluded. What is there in the anecdote that the biography cannot capture? What critical purchase is lost when the order in which Shakespeare wrote his works replaces that of the classical dramatic genres? What do compendia offer that the authorial archive cannot recognize? What happens to the attractions of a miscellany in the insatiable quest for the first-person? To ask these questions is to begin to loosen the grip biography has long held over the works. It is to entertain a fact that otherwise seems almost unthinkable. For a long spell between 1616 and 1800, Shakespeare's plays and poems were reproduced, discussed, and valued without a biographical narrative. Not only were his works not desperately in need of a biography; they were surviving then perfectly well without one—perhaps all the better for the lack of one.

1
Shakespeare without a Life (1564–1616)

For over two centuries after his death in 1616, Shakespeare had no Life. Let me begin by defining what I mean by Life: I mean a continuous narrative from birth to death, chronologically organized and supported by documents. No such narrative prefaced the four seventeenth-century folio editions of his collected plays, *Mr. William Shakespeares Comedies, Histories, & Tragedies* (1623, 1632, 1663/4, and 1685). Instead, the front matter of all four massive folio volumes dwelled on his death. Not until the first eighteenth-century edition are the folio's elegiac preliminaries replaced with a prefatory Life. Nicholas Rowe's six-volume octavo edition of *The Works of Mr. William Shakespear* (1709) opens with a forty-page essay, *Some Account of the Life &c. of Mr. William Shakespear*, and that essay continues to be reproduced in a succession of Shakespeare editions up through the end of the century.[1] But Rowe's prefatory Life of Shakespeare is quite unlike the biographies that subsequently made their way into the standard editions of Shakespeare's Complete Works. It pieces together discrete anecdotes and comments rather than attempting a coherent narrative, pays scant attention to chronology, and relies on what has been said about Shakespeare without recourse to documents and records.

My definition of a Life could be still more concise. Shakespeare had no Life that conformed to the bracketed biographical formula that appears in this chapter's title: "(1564–1616)." The formula is abstract: two dated endpoints, of birth and of death, are connected by a long dash that stands for the lifetime between them; parentheses set it off as a self-contained unit. The abbreviation is now standard, but it became so only after the publication of *Dictionary of National Biography* (*DNB*) at the end of the nineteenth century (1885–1900). Each of that publication's 30,000 entries opens with the subject's name followed by the parenthetical life dates. The ensuing biographical narrative for each of those entries is a dilation of that formula. It has been the conventional abbreviation for a Life ever since, including in the *Oxford Dictionary of National Biography* (*ODNB*), completed in 2004 and, when combined with its online supplements, containing almost twice as many entries as the *DNB*. Until the turn of the twentieth century, there was no such convention of biographical notation in England. It does not feature in early biographical compendia, like John Aubrey's *Brief Lives*, Samuel Johnson's *Lives of the Poets*, or the comprehensive *Biographia Britannica of Eminent Persons*, the precursor of the *Dictionary of National Biography*. Nor is the formula to be found on early modern tombstones or monuments. In his stately folio volume of *Ancient Funerall Monuments* (1631), John Weever recorded some one thousand inscriptions on tombs and gravestones, mainly in southeast England, but they give only the year of death or burial; the same is true of the epitaphs John Stow lists in his *The Survey of London* (1598).[2] Instead of a date range, we find *hic iacet, qui obit, quis obit,* or *obiit Anno domini* followed by the death date, or occasionally *aetatis* followed by the age at death. This is customary throughout the seventeenth and early eighteenth centuries. If the birth-date appears, as is the case on Edmund Spenser's monument, it is the result of a later inscription.[3] Anthony Wood's remarkable folio *Athenae Oxonienses* claims on its title page to give "The Birth, Fortune, Preferment, and Death" of all the authors and prelates who have been educated at Oxford, but by "Birth" he means not date of birth, but parentage, lineage, or place of birth.[4]

***

Birthdates are lacking during this early period not because they are nowhere to be found. As Adam Smyth has noted, by Thomas Cromwell's edict of 1538, the recording of both baptismal and burial dates in parish registers was mandatory.[5] The baptismal and burial dates for any parishioner who lived into adulthood would also be separated by records of intervening parish christenings, marriages, and burials. Shakespeare's two dates, for example, in the Stratford parish register, are separated by over eighty pages (5r to 46v). His baptism is entered in Latin on 26 April 1564: "Guilielmus filius Johannes Shakspere"; his burial in English: "25th of April 1616."[6] For any individual baptized and buried in the same parish, it would have taken only a little patience to ascertain the extent of a lifespan by conjoining the two dates. But there appears to have been no incentive to do so. The death date is what mattered: the date marking the cut-off point between this world and the next, between life and afterlife.[7] Shakespeare's burial site became a landmark shortly after his death; there is no record of his birth place on Henley Street until a surveyor notes it in 1759.[8]

While no dates appear on Shakespeare's gravestone in Holy Trinity Church in Stratford, there is one on the bronze plaque at the base of the funerary monument above it (Fig. 1.1).

Fig. 1.1 Shakespeare's funerary monument, Holy Trinity Church, Stratford-upon-Avon, with details of memorial plaque and of obit.

A few decades later, that inscription and the monument were reproduced in an engraving based on the drawing of the antiquarian William Dugdale (Fig. 1.2).

The engraving commemorates Shakespeare not as the Warwickshire poet who lived from 1564 to 1616, but as the one who died in 1616 at the age of 53. His birthdate does appear on Shakespeare's monument

Fig. 1.2 Engraving of Shakespeare's funerary monument by Wenceslaus Hollar, in William Dugdale, *The Antiquities of Warwickshire Illustrated* (1656), with detail of obit.

erected in 1741 in the "Poets' Corner" of Westminster Abbey, but it was not added until 1977.

Early biographical entries for Shakespeare also supply only the date of death.[9] In his *Brief Lives*, John Aubrey does his best to obtain dates of birth, for the purpose of casting horoscopes for his subjects, what he terms "genitures" or "nativities," though he succeeds for only a fraction of his subjects.[10] Two early compendia of lives give no year even for Shakespeare's death, only the century. In *The History of the Worthies of England* (1662) Thomas Fuller records: "He dyed *Anno Domini* 16 ... and was buried at Stratford upon Avon."[11] William Winstanley, in his *The Lives of the Most Famous English Poets* (1687), reproduces Fuller's ellipsis: "This our famous Comedian died, *An. Dom.* 16__ and was buried at *Stratford* upon *Avon*."[12] Gerard Langbaine, in his *An Account of the English Dramatick Poets* (1691), lifts Shakespeare's death date from Dugdale's engraving: "I have now no more to do, but to close up all, with an Account of his Death; which was on the 23d of April, An. Dom. 16. ..."[13]

When annotating his copy of Langbaine's survey of English dramatists, the antiquary William Oldys notes that Langbaine's entry on Shakespeare derives from Dugdale and then calculates Shakespeare's birthdate on that entry's basis. By subtracting "Aet. 53" from "Obit An. Dom. 1616," Oldys arrives at 1563.[14] Several decades later, Edmond Malone transcribes Oldys's notes into his own interleaved copy of Langbaine and inserts many of his own, including a correction of Oldys's calculation: "He was born in 1564. [Dugdale's] inscription led Oldys into the mistake" (Fig. 1.3).[15]

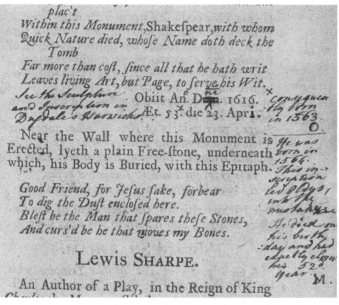

Fig. 1.3 Edmond Malone's manuscript correction of William Oldys's note on Shakespeare's birthdate, in Malone's interleaved copy of Gerard Langbaine, *An Account of the English Dramatick Poets* (1691). © Bodleian Libraries, University of Oxford.

By the eighteenth century, the Stratford parish register recording the date of Shakespeare's baptism had been consulted. Rowe, in preparation for writing his 1709 Life of Shakespeare, had sent the actor Thomas Betterton to Warwickshire "on purpose to gather what Remains he could" of Shakespeare. It is in Rowe's *Some Account of the Life, & c.* that the month and year of Shakespeare's birth is finally first made known: "Born at *Stratford* upon *Avon,* in *Warwickshire* in *April* 1564."[16]

But Malone wants the day of Shakespeare's birth as well as the month and year. The day supplied by the register—April 26, 1564—is of Shakespeare's baptism. For the absence of this desiderata, Malone faults the period's record-keeping practices: "The omitting to mention of the day of the child's birth in baptismal registers, is a great defect, as the knowledge of this fact is often of importance." Yet as far as the parish was concerned, the important date would have been that in which infants received the sacrament that adopted them into the Christian community. What Malone wants was never documented: the precise starting point of his subject's life. He begrudgingly must take the day of birth on trust, from one of his correspondents, the Stratford vicar and schoolmaster Joseph Greene: "William Shakespeare was born in Stratford upon Avon, *probably* on Sunday, April the 23d, 1564." As he later reflects, "I have said this on faith of Mr. Green, but *quaere,* how did Mr. Green ascertain this fact?"[17]

That Malone should be so keen to fix both dates is no accident, for he is the first to attempt a continuous, chronological, and documented Life of Shakespeare, comprehending his works and extending from his birth to his death. As we shall see, he falls far short of that ideal and his biography consisting of 500 densely annotated pages of text and over 200 pages of appendices, though no doubt consulted as a reference, was not reprinted.[18] The first biography fully to realize Malone's aspiration was by Sidney Lee who, in his capacity as first assistant to the editor of the *DNB* and finally as its editor, wrote a total of 870 entries. In 1898 he contributes a forty-nine-page entry on "Shakespeare, William (1564–1616)," the longest by far in the Dictionary. Lee's entry, organized chronologically, forms the basis of what he would expand the following year into his 500-page *A Life of William Shakespeare.* In 1916, after five editions, his biography was enlarged, revised, and proclaimed the standard biography.[19] It is also the prototype for the biographical accounts that preface modern editions of the Complete or the Collected Works of Shakespeare. But throughout most of the eighteenth century, the Life of Shakespeare prefixed to the works has no use for the *DNB*'s epitaphic or biographic formula. Rowe's

Some Account of the Life, & c. is without continuity or development and no documents substantiate the incidents it relates.

***

The first comprehensive collection of Shakespeare's plays, the 1623 Folio and its three seventeenth-century reprints, is prefaced not with an account of Shakespeare's life but with several notices of his death, in prose and verse.[20] The preliminaries stress the volume's posthumous status. Consistently, they sever the dead author from the works he has left behind. The title-page engraving of Shakespeare, generally considered "stiff" and "lifeless," has been likened to an effigy on a sepulchral memorial. It has recently been suggested that Droeshout's portrait is intended to evoke a death mask, and that the poem across from it, "To the Reader," attributed to Ben Jonson, awakens the etymological link between the engraver or "Grauer" who cut the brass and the gravemaker.[21] Jonson's short ekphrastic verse diverts the reader's attention from the graven image of Shakespeare to the printed text of his book: "Reader, looke / Not on his Picture, but his Booke."[22] John Heminges and Henry Condell, Shakespeare's theatrical colleagues and the compilers of the Folio, insist on the same separation in both their dedication to the Earls of Pembroke and Montgomery and in their address to the reader: the author is dead and buried; his works, however, live on within the protective covers of the book. Ideally, the compilers maintain, Shakespeare would have overseen its publication: "It had bene a thing, we confesse, worthie to have bene wished, that the *Author* himselfe had liv'd to have set forth, and overseen his owne *writings.*" Not having done so, like a man who has died intestate, his two colleagues take it upon themselves to secure the future of his dramatic legacy: "he by death departed from that right, we pray you do not envie his Friends, the office of their care, and paine, to have collected & publish'd them." Heminges and Condell dutifully perform "an office to the dead." With his physical body interred, their duty is to safeguard the literary corpus he has left behind. The corpus that survives him has suffered in his absence: "abus'd," "expos'd," "maimed and deformed": scattered like the dismembered body of Orpheus or the mangled remnants of Osiris. But through his executors' solicitude, that broken and dispersed corpus has been made whole again, "cur'd, and perfect of their *limbes*," now enclosed within the protective covers of the mighty Folio, the tomb of the voluminous tome.[23]

Still more is needed to secure the survival of his literary remains, and again the postmortem caesura is emphasized. During the author's lifetime, the titled dedicatees of the volume, the Earls of Pembroke and Montgomery, had looked after both the parent author and his poetic issue: back then they "prosequted both [his works], and their Authour liuing." But now with "our Authour no longer living," his patrons must attend to his surviving issue: "we hope, (that [the plays] out-liuing him, and he not having the fate, common with some, to be exequtor to his own writings) you will use the like indulgence toward them, you have done unto their parent."[24] It is no longer the author who needs patronage, but the publication that will secure the survival of his dramatic issue. In sum, Shakespeare is dead and gone. Long live "what he has left," the "remaines of your servant *Shakespeare*": his *Comedies, Histories, & Tragedies.*

By contributing elegies to the book's front matter, the fellow poets of the deceased also perform "an office to the dead," mourning Shakespeare's departure while welcoming the survival of his writing. The tributes are less commendatory verses, as they are often called, than commemorative.[25] They are written *in memoriam:* "To the memory of my beloued, The Author" (Jonson); "To the memorie of M. W. Shakespeare" (Mabbes); "To the memory of the deceased Authour" (Leonard Digges). Hugh Holland's chiasmic line nicely encapsulates the volume's premise: "for done are *Shakespeares* dayes: / His dayes are done."[26] The 1632 Folio introduces two more elegies, both unattributed, "Upon the Effigies of ... Shakespeare" and "An Epitaph on ... Shakespeare."[27] On the closing leaf of a copy of the First Folio, its early owner inscribed an additional three epitaphs: "An Epitaph on Mr. William Shakespeare"; "Another upon the same"; "an Epitaph (vpon his Toombe stone incised)."[28]

As the massive folio had collected Shakespeare's far-flung plays in 1623 and 1632, so a very small octavo, *Poems: Written by Wil. Shake-speare*, purported to do the same on a reduced scale with his poems in 1640, collecting verses that had appeared in different publications associated with Shakespeare's name.[29] Its publisher's desire to affiliate the octavo with the Folio is apparent in its frontispiece (Fig. 1.4): an engraving based on the Droeshout portrait on the Folio's frontispiece, now looking even less alive than in the original, with a ghostly aureole behind his head:

This Shadowe is renowned Shakespear's: Soule of th'age
The applause? delight! the wonder of the Stage.
Nature her selfe, was proud of his designes
And joy'd to weare the dressing of his lines,
The learned will Confess, his workes are such,
As neither man, nor Muse, can prayse to much.
For ever live thy fame, the world to tell,
Thy like, no age, shall ever paralell.
                                              W.M. sculpsit.

Fig. 1.4 Engraving of Shakespeare by William Marshall, frontispiece to John Benson's *Poems: Written by Wil. Shake-speare. Gent.* (1640). © Folger Shakespeare Library.

"This Shadow is renowned Shakespear's," reads the inscription.

Like the folios, too, the octavo aims to attend to the "offices of the dead" by gathering the author's literary remains so that the poems might enjoy "proportionale glory, with the rest of his *everliving Workes*."[30] Elegiac tributes enclose the poems attributed to Shakespeare, two eulogies at the front (by Leonard Digges and John Warren) and three at the end (by John Milton, William Basse, and an anonymous poet). Here, too, the verses emphasize the distinction between the deceased poet and his surviving works. In Leonard Digges's eulogy, Shakespeare the "deceased man" is survived by his works in the form not of print but of the stage: by the host of ravishing personae, among them Brutus, Iago, Falstaff, Beatrice, Benedict, and "Malvoglio that crosse garter'd Gull." Milton, in his "*An Epitaph* on the admirable Dramaticke Poet, William Shakespeare," imagines the works living on in still another locus: in readers' hearts, where his lines will be deeply impressed or "Sepulcher'd." The focus of the most widely disseminated of the elegies from either collection is on the location of Shakespeare's physical body. William Basse's "On the Death of William Shakespeare, who Died in Aprill, *Anno. Dom. 1616*" references both the Westminster tomb of Chaucer, Spenser, and Beaumont, where Shakespeare does not lie, and the Stratford monument, where he does lie, the elegy's lines a transcription of the epitaphic *requiescat in pace*: "Under this carved marble of thine owne, / Sleepe rare Tragoedian Shakespeare, sleepe alone."[31]

The preliminaries to both the 1623 Folio of *Mr. William Shakespeares Comedies, Histories, & Tragedies* and the 1640 octavo of *Poems: Written by Wil. Shake-speare. Gent.* feature no homage to Shakespeare's life. Nor does the only front matter of another verse collection, the 1609 quarto of *Shakes-peare's Sonnets*. As Chapter 4 will discuss, the quarto's dedication is set to resemble an epitaph in stone, though at the time of its publication in 1609, Shakespeare was very much alive. All three publications open by foregrounding Shakespeare's decease, marking off different destinations for the man and his work, the former enclosed by the tomb and the latter by the tome.[32] The life of the one ends in 1616, while that of the others begins with the date of publication: 1623, 1640, 1609 respectively.

Without a prefatory Life, there is no invitation to read the ensuing dramatic and poetic content biographically. The key date is of publication, the date when the plays or poems take on a life in print; their date of issue is independent of their authorial genesis. "[N]ow that the author is no longer living," as the Folio puts it, his works can survive on their own. Rescued by the efforts of their solicitous compilers and sanctioned by the titles of their two powerful patrons, the plays take their leave of the author, much as the soul after death departs from the body in the hope of crossing the threshold to eternal life. The poetry also aspires to immortality, or at least its qualified worldly equivalent: survival until doomsday, as the couplet of sonnet 55 asserts: "So, till the judgment that yourself arise, / You live in this, and dwell in lovers' eyes."[33]

When we say "Shakespeare," we might intend either the person or his corpus. The 1623 Folio and the 1640 octavo, however, distinguish between the two: the life of one is over; the life of the other endures. *Ars longa, vita brevis*. At the portal to their publication, the works are severed from Shakespeare by death rather than sutured to him by a Life.

***

In 1709 Shakespeare's works were published for the first time with a preliminary Life. Nicholas Rowe's edition of *The Works of Mr. William Shakespear* begins with his forty-page essay *Some Account of the Life, & c.* But his Life certainly does not satisfy my working definition. At the start of his account Rowe gives the date of Shakespeare's baptism from the parish register; at its end he transcribes his age at death from the monument, but what lies between those dates is not "the first attempt at a connected biography of Shakespeare," as Samuel Schoenbaum claims in *Shakespeare's Lives*.[34] Rowe's focus is on Shakespeare's working life, the period in which he was active (*floruit* or *fl.*), beginning with his departure from Stratford to London and ending with his return. Between these two undated termini are incidents relating to Shakespeare's encounters in London, also undated. Rowe relates them not in chronological order, but in the order of the social rank of the persons Shakespeare encounters. The first is the Queen, then Southampton, and then come the "private men": Spenser first, then Jonson and his tribe, whose members are also listed in order of rank: Sir John Suckling, Sir William Davenant, Sir Endymion Porter, the cleric John Hales, and last of all, Ben Jonson (once apprenticed to a bricklayer). Rowe's anecdotes are now familiar and yet their structural similarity has gone unremarked. In none of them is there development. Shakespeare's behavior remains unchanged—or rather his *mis*behavior: again and again he breaks social, legal, and ethical protocols. And each offence has some form of literary outcome.

Rowe's first anecdote tells of the "Misfortune" that launches Shakespeare's literary career. In Stratford he is caught poaching deer, or as Rowe puts it less glamorously, "robbing a Park" or "Deer stealing" in an "ill Company" of "young Fellows"—and repeatedly, "more than once".[35] The landowner prosecutes Shakespeare, who compounds the offence with a defamatory ballad protesting his punishment. The ballad is so "very bitter" that the landowner redoubles his prosecution, forcing Shakespeare to flee his native Stratford for London. Rowe chooses his words carefully to describe Shakespeare's infraction: he calls it "an Extravagance that he was guilty of." "Extravagance" here sticks close to its Latin roots (*extra*, beyond + *vagari*, to wander), as is evident in John Kersey's *A New English Dictionary* (1702), where it is defined as "wandering beyond the due bounds" and given the following synonyms: "disordinate," "irregular," "wild," "savage," "furious."[36] As we shall see, in the anecdotes Shakespeare repeatedly, indeed chronically, goes "beyond the due bounds." By trespassing and stealing, he oversteps the limits of the law, as he does again with his libelous ballad, conjectured to be his first literary effort.[37] This occasion, Rowe adds with his usual delicacy, temporarily "put a Blemish upon [Shakespeare's] good Manners" and obliged him to leave Warwickshire and "for some time, shelter himself in *London*." Samuel Johnson is more direct: "terrour of a criminal prosecution" forced his flight.[38]

As his writing career began with offence in Stratford, so does it end there, also in offence. "[S]ome Years before his Death" (xxxv), Rowe tells us, in a gathering of friends and neighbors, one of his closest, a Mr. Combe, well known for his "Wealth and Usury" (xxxvi), asks Shakespeare—"in a laughing manner"—to write his epitaph, eager to know how he will be remembered. Shakespeare obliges, but hardly in the genial spirit of the request. He extemporizes an epitaph that gives Combe first only a ten percent chance of salvation (the usurious rate at which Combe had been lending)—"*Tis a Hundred to Ten, his Soul is not sav'd*"—and then drops that to no chance at all, for Combe is already in hell: "*If any Man ask, Who lies in this Tomb?/Oh! ho! quoth the Devil, 'tis my John-a-Combe*" (xxxvi). It is a breach of decorum, to be sure, and no doubt casts a pall over a convivial occasion. It is also a terrible way to treat a friend. Rowe characteristically refrains from direct censure, though his concluding statement tells where his sympathies lie: "[T]he Sharpness of the Satyr is said to have stung the Man so severely, that he never forgave it." Later ages have done their best to turn both of these "personal stor[ies]" (i) to Shakespeare's advantage, arguing, for example, that in stealing deer, Shakespeare was protesting enclosure laws or that in damning Combe, he was excoriating the practice of usury. But Rowe's

Shakespeare has no such political or social conscience. His career begins and ends in injury to others, resulting in a libelous ballad at the start and a blasphemous satire at the end. Between these two telling offences are more of the same.

Even to his queen, Shakespeare is insolent, if not insubordinate. She, displeased with his having given his old fat rogue the name of the Protestant martyr Sir John Oldcastle, "was pleas'd to command him to alter it." He does alter it, but to a name of equal rank and virtue, another Sir John, a Knight of the Garter and war hero, Sir John Falstaff. "The present Offence was indeed avoided," Rowe allows, though not without reservation: "I don't know whether the Author may not have been somewhat to blame in his second Choice" (ix). Shakespeare may have obeyed the letter of her command, but certainly not its intent of protecting her knights' reputation.

With his patron, the Earl of Southampton, comes another tale of immoderation. In an act of "profuse Generosity," Southampton gives the dramatist a thousand pounds: "A Bounty very great, and very rare at any time," adds Rowe. Yet this inordinate sum is not, as might be expected from a patron, to encourage Shakespeare's literary endeavors. Rather, it is "to enable [Shakespeare] to go through with a Purchase which [the Earl] heard he had a mind to." Rowe leaves the reader wondering what Shakespeare might have had the mind to buy for such an exorbitant sum. Perhaps Rowe intends to hint at it when he tells what the sum could purchase in his own day: it is, Rowe mentions, "almost equal to that profuse Generosity the present Age has shewn to *French* Dancers and *Italian* Eunuchs" (x).[39]

Among the anecdotes not included in Rowe is one recorded in Shakespeare's lifetime by John Manningham, then studying law at the Inns of Court. In his diary entry dated March 13, 1601, he tells how Shakespeare preempted Richard Burbage's late night tryst with a female admirer: William "at his game" when Richard's arrival was announced, justified his precedence with the quip, "William the Conqueror was before Richard the Third."[40] A later anecdote, first noted by John Aubrey, alludes to another illicit liaison. Shakespeare, according to Aubrey, in journeying to and from London to Stratford, would stop off at a tavern where the vintner's wife, "a very beautifull woman, and of a very good witt and of conversation extremely agreable" was William Davenant's mother.[41] These circumstances gave rise to the rumor, fostered by Davenant himself, that Davenant was not only Shakespeare's namesake and protégé but also his illegitimate son. Thus adultery could be added to the litany of Shakespeare's offences: robbery, libel, treason (in disobeying his monarch's command, and blasphemy. In this context, it seems only fitting that the alleged cause of Shakespeare's death should be intemperance. John Ward, vicar of Stratford parish from 1662, jotted in his notebooks that "Shakespeare, Drayton and Ben Jonson had a merry meeting, and it seems drank too hard, for Shakespeare died of a fever there contracted."[42] An inglorious death, to be sure, but excess of drink and high blood pressure are certainly in keeping with a lifetime of incontinence. So, too, perhaps, is the malediction carved on his gravestone, reputed to have been composed by Shakespeare shortly before his death, damning—in the name of Jesus, no less—whatever hapless sexton were to be charged with making room for new corpses: "cursed be he that moves my bones."[43] If the epitaph were indeed by Shakespeare, it would constitute the only writing we have in his own person besides the Sonnets. It would also qualify as his last piece of writing, displacing the more propitious The Tempest, long held to be Shakespeare's valedictory work.[44]

But what motivates these consistently negative characterizations? Certainly not the documentary record. It suggests just the opposite, at least as it is available and interpreted now. As Stephen Greenblatt observes, "The fact that there are no police reports, no privy council orders, indictments, or post-mortem inquests" suggests that Shakespeare "possessed a gift for staying out of trouble."[45] (In short, had he been less law-abiding, he would have left more records behind. Unlike so many of his playhouse cohort—Marlowe, Kyd, Nashe, Jonson, Middleton, and Dekker all spent time in prison—Shakespeare avoided scrapes with the law.[46] When dated biographical narratives replace the discrete anecdotes, Shakespeare's character takes on a new respectability. Malone's biography, The Life of William Shakspeare, intended from its inception "to weave the whole into one uniform and connected narrative," sets out to show that Shakespeare "from his youth upwards, demonstrated that respectability of character which unquestionably belonged to him in after life."[47] Its aim, at least in theory, was to follow a trajectory in which his developing talent as a dramatist is matched by gradual acquisition of property, literary acclaim, social status, and appreciation and affection of family, colleagues, and friends: a life well lived and justly rewarded.

So, the question remains: why is the anecdotal Shakespeare at such variance from the Shakespeare of later narratives?

***

Shakespeare's character in these anecdotes may be at odds with the documentary record, but it is very much in keeping with his writing, as assessed by his early critics. "Extravagant," "unruly," and "irregular" crop up repeatedly in criticism of his plays. Rowe is solicitous not to be seen to contribute to this critique: "I would not be thought by this to mean, that his Fancy was so loose and extravagant, as to be Independent on the Rule and Government of Judgment" (vii). And yet he repeatedly suggests the same. He notes that Shakespeare took his plots as he finds them in his sources—rambling romances and sprawling chronicles—without attending to "the fit Disposition, Order, and Conduct" required of a dramatic plot (xxvii). He charges *The Merchant of Venice* with offending "the Rules of Probability" with "that extravagant and unusual kind of Bond" that stipulates a pound of flesh for defaulting on a loan (xx). *The Tempest* is the exception to Shakespeare's legendary neglect of the unities: "the Unities are kept there with an Exactness uncommon to the Liberties of his Writing" (xxiii). Only when Shakespeare quits the natural world is his extravagance a virtue: then he "gives his Imagination *an entire Loose* and raises his Fancy to a flight *above* Mankind and the *Limits* of the visible world" (xxii, italics added). Thus, Rowe applauds the faeries of *A Midsummer Night's Dream*, the sprites of *The Tempest*, the witches of *Macbeth*, the ghost in *Hamlet* as examples of the "beautiful Extravagance which we admire in *Shakespear*" (iii), a judgment that a stricter neoclassicist, Charles Gildon, found bafflingly self-contradictory: "I cannot imagine; nor do I understand what is meant by *Beautiful Extravagance.*" For poetry unregulated by "the Rules of Art," and therefore exceeding the bounds of nature, "can never be *Beautiful* but *Abominable.*"[48]

For Rowe, while extravagance mars plot, it can enhance character, as with the "extravagant Character of *Caliban* ... a wonderful Invention, a particular wild image ... one of the finest and most uncommon Grotesques that was ever seen" (xxiv); the excessively melancholic Jacques; "the fantastical Steward *Malvolio*" (xix); and the "irregular Greatness of Mind in *M. Antony*" (xxx). But it is Falstaff, "allow'd by every body to be a Master-piece" (xvii), who outdoes the others in extravagances: theft, lies, cowardice, vain-glory, "and in short, every way Vicious" (xviii). He also possesses too much wit and this, according to Rowe, is Shakespeare's doing. He has "given him so much Wit as to make him almost too agreeable," so that audiences are inclined to lament his banishment by the newly coronated king. "Wit" is also the faculty Shakespeare has in abundance, as is emphasized by Rowe's repeated references to it: "the advantages of his Wit" (viii); "the Reputation of his Wit" (ix); "the power of his Wit" (x). And indeed, his wit, without the critic's caveats, poses the same danger as Falstaff's: its attraction is irresistible.

Rowe does identify one play in which Shakespeare exercises uncharacteristic restraint and thereby for once outshines the ancients. Though Hamlet's motives for abhorring his mother, "heighten'd by Incest," are greater than those of Orestes, Shakespeare, unlike Sophocles, "restrains [his protagonist] from doing Violence to his Mother" and "makes his Father's Ghost forbid that part of his Vengeance" (xxxiii). For once, Shakespeare holds back and thereby proves more measured and correct than his venerated ancient counterpart.

While Rowe is careful to offset his criticism of Shakespeare with praise, he gives his essay's final critical word to a less genial (and far more influential) earlier critic. Ben Jonson had allowed that "There was ever more in [Shakespeare] to be Prais'd than to be Pardon'd." Yet as Rowe astutely points out, Jonson's praise of Shakespeare is hardly unqualified: "if at times he has affected to commend [Shakespeare], it has always been with some Reserve, insinuating his Uncorrectness, a careless manner of Writing, and want of Judgment" (xiii). In the page-length passage Rowe quotes from Jonson's *Discoveries* (xxxviii–xxxix), Jonson repeatedly informs his praise with an all but revoking qualification, as in his decree that "His Wit was in his own Power, would the Rule of it had been so too." In the same passage, his admiration for Shakespeare's "[e]xcellent Fancy, brave Notions, and gentle Expressions" is clouded by his disdain for his lack of self-control: "he flow'd with that Facility, that sometimes it was necessary he should be stopp'd: *Sufflaminandus erat*, as *Augustus* said of *Haterius*." Jonson faults the two compilers of the 1623 Folio for praising what he sees as the telltale sign of Shakespeare's stylistic impetuosity. In their address to the reader, Heminges and Condell may well have been promoting their folio texts of the plays over those previously published in quarto when they boast of the pristine state of the manuscripts from which they were printed, "And what he thought, he uttered with that easinesse, that wee have scarse received from him a blot in his papers."[49] Jonson, however, chooses to interpret it as praise for Shakespeare's stylistic license which he resoundingly condemns: "Would he had blotted a thousand." The rebuke, he insists, is intended not to offend but to instruct, lest Shakespeare's prospective readers take Shakespeare's salient defect for a virtue: "I had not told Posterity this, but for [Heminges and Condell's] Ignorance, who chose that Circumstance to commend their Friend by, wherein he most faulted."[50]

In the classical tradition, for Horace and Seneca, for example, the absence of blots signals haste and carelessness in composition: the *currente calamo* or writing "with a running pen" that knows no discipline. Blots are evidence of deliberation, of the work of rethinking and revising. Pope, in his epistle in imitation of Horace, blames not only Shakespeare for not blotting but also John Dryden:

> And fluent Shakespeare scarce effac'd a line.
> Ev'n copious Dryden, wanted, or forgot,
> The last and greatest Art, the Art to blot.[51]

In this critical tradition, Shakespeare never mastered "the art to blot." Rowe's quote includes Jonson's translation of Seneca's description of the orator Haterius, who spoke so incessantly—that is, non-stop—that the Emperor Augustus himself had to bring him to a halt. By contrast, Jonson's translation of this description is heavily punctuated, evidence of his attention to the logical, rhetorical, and semantic prescripts he outlines in the final chapter of his *The English Grammar*.[52]

A century later, Samuel Johnson criticized Shakespeare for the same impetuousness: "an author not systematick and consequential, but desultory and vagrant."[53] A lover of anecdotes, Johnson must have taken particular pleasure in adding to Rowe's *Some Account* one of the wittiest and raciest sendups of Shakespeare's signature unruliness. In Johnson's retelling, Shakespeare, running from the law, finds employment in London as what Johnson terms "a waiter," holding the horses of play-goers at the playhouse gate for a few hours while they enjoyed the performance. His skill as groom was noted, so that "in a short time every man as he alighted called for Will. Shakespeare, and scarcely any other waiter was trusted with a horse while Will. Shakespeare could be had." The demand for his service was overwhelming:

> Shakespeare finding more horses put into his hand than he could hold, hired boys to wait under his inspection, who, when Will. Shakespeare was summoned, were immediately to present themselves, "I am Shakespeare's boy, Sir". In time Shakespeare found higher employment, but as long as the practice of riding to the playhouse continued, the waiters that held the horses retained the appellation of Shakespeare's boys.[54]

Later biographies, keen for material to fill the gap between Shakespeare's departure from Stratford and his arrival in London, have either dismissed this account as "pure nonsense" or taken it as early evidence of Shakespeare's entrepreneurial spirit. Yet might not the story relate to his reputation for writing *currente calamo*? As the anecdote maintains, even after Shakespeare found "higher employment" as a celebrated dramatist, his name was associated with the boys who helped him with the horses he could not control.

As Rowe had suggested at the start of his Life of Shakespeare, "the knowledge of an Authour may sometimes conduce to the better understanding his Book." Shakespeare's style, plots, and characters are illuminated by incidents foregrounding his free-wheeling misconduct. We might then call Rowe's Life a literary biography. Indeed, the full title of his essay, as advertised by the title page to the 1709 edition, makes the connection between Shakespeare's life and works explicit: *An Account of the Life and Writings of the Author*, though later abbreviated as *Some Account of the Life, &c.* Shakespeare's biographers have always been tempted to draw on the anecdotes, however tangentially, for any measure of truth pertaining to the events of Shakespeare's life or the facets of his character. But these stories are less about Shakespeare the man who lived from 1564 to 1616 than about the literary corpus that survived his death. So, too, there is the temptation to work these anecdotes into the biographical narrative, to slot them into the chronological continuum, as if each were a piece of the biographical whole. The mistake here is categorical, for each anecdote is a unit unto itself, intended to circulate on its own. When strung together, in whatever order, the anecdotes form no narrative, only variations on the same theme, each leaving the same impression of Shakespeare's character: at best rude and brash, at worst criminal and sacrilegious. Rowe collects first the incidents relating to his flouting of social mores and then moves on to his neglect of literary decorum. "The character of the man is best seen in his writing" (xxxvii), concludes Rowe, bringing the essay full circle. The man and his work share the same character: a lack of discipline evident in both an unmannerly life and an indecorous style.

***

As we shall see in the next chapter, Edmond Malone, the first biographer of Shakespeare (1564–1616), took pride and pleasure in invalidating Rowe's Life with documentary evidence: "My plan will have the advantage of novelty, for I think I shall be able to overturn every received tradition respecting this very extraordinary man."[55] But there was one tradition pertaining to Shakespeare that was impossible to disprove: his alleged unfamiliarity with the ancients. As Johnson observed in the preface to his edition: "There has always prevailed a tradition, that Shakespeare wanted learning, that he had no regular education, nor much skill in the dead languages."[56] In this case, it is not evidence but the lack of it that is incontrovertible. Shakespeare's name does not appear in the record of matriculants at Oxford and Cambridge. There is no evidence that his formal schooling went beyond his Stratford grammar school education. Not having attended university, his knowledge of the ancient tongues and the works written in them was judged de facto to be inadequate, at least for a poet and dramatist. How could poems and plays be written without full and deep knowledge of the ancient models and rules that defined the genres?

Unlike Shakespeare, the major playwrights of his day were scholars, having attended either Oxford or Cambridge: John Lyly, Robert Greene, Thomas Lodge, George Peele, Christopher Marlowe, Thomas Nashe, Thomas Middleton, Francis Beaumont, and John Fletcher. Their advanced formal study of the ancient tongues and works qualified them to write in imitation of them in their own vulgar tongue. Humphrey Moseley, the publisher of the 1647 folio of Beaumont and Fletcher's plays, held it to be "a knowne Truth" that both playwrights possessed not only the "high unexpressible gifts of *Nature*, but also excellent *acquired Parts*, being furnished with Arts and Sciences by that liberall education they had at the *University*, which sure is the best place to make a great Wit understand it selfe."[57] Thomas Kyd and Ben Jonson did not attend university, but both studied under illustrious tutors—Kyd under Richard Mulcaster, the headmaster of the Merchant Taylors School, and Jonson under William Camden, headmaster of Westminster School. Even so, Kyd is among those whom Thomas Nashe ridicules for busying themselves with "the indevors of Art that could scarcely latinize their necke-verse," that is, lacking the modicum of Latin required to exempt criminals from hanging: the reading of Psalm 51 from the Vulgate, *Miserere mei, Deus.*[58] This was no problem for Ben Jonson, of course, the English Horace renowned for his scholarship and his mastery of classical genres, who famously escaped the charge of manslaughter by claiming benefit of clergy.

In the earliest known allusion to him in print, Shakespeare is quite explicitly an outcast among university playwrights. A letter included in the pamphlet *Greene's Groatsworth of Wit* (1592), written by (or as if by) Robert Greene on his deathbed and addressed to three "fellow scholars about the city"—now identified as Christopher Marlowe, Thomas

Nashe, and George Peele—warns of one player in particular who has presumed to write plays:

> [T]here is an upstart Crow, beautified with our feathers, that with his *Tygers hart wrapt in a Players hyde*, supposes he is as well able to bombast out a blanke verse as the best of you: and beeing an absolute *Iohannes fac totum*, is in his owne conceit the onely Shake-scene in a countrey.[59]

In reviling Shakespeare as an "upstart Crow," a raucous countryside bird, the bane of farmers, Greene is unlikely to be disparaging Shakespeare's provincial origins, for his own background was hardly less humble; probably born in Norwich, his father was said to be a saddler or cordwainer turned innkeeper. But Greene, like his three "fellow scholars," had attended university before making his move to London and a literary career, while Shakespeare remained rustically at home in Stratford. (The anecdotes keep his rusticity in view through association with animals, casting him as the son of a wool-dealer or of a butcher in whose shop he slays calves while declaiming in high style, a poacher of deer and rabbits, a groom holding horses.) Greene instead protests the player-turned-playwright's presumption in plucking feathers or *pennae*/pennings from his literary betters.[60] Greene's charge here may not be, as is often assumed, that Shakespeare has filched from the works of others (what poet of the time did not?), but that he presumed to write drama without the requisite university credentials.[61] Indeed Greene may have intended the line from *3 Henry VI* he parodies—"O tiger's heart, wrapped in a woman's hide"[62]—as just such a purloined feather. As recent critics have noted, Queen Margaret mocks York with his son's death in *3 Henry VI* as Medea had taunted Jason after slaughtering his sons in both Euripides' and Seneca's tragedies of *Medea*.[63] Like Margaret, Medea is termed a tiger by both, as she also is in John Studley's translation of Seneca, which Shakespeare is believed to have consulted.[64]

In a verse letter to Ben Jonson, Francis Beaumont, feigning untutored modesty in addressing his formidable mentor, compares his own low style first to that of a Devon cheesemaker and then to Shakespeare: "heere, I would lett slipp / (If I had any in me) schollershipp, / And from all learninge leaue these lines as cleare / As *Shakespeares* best are."[65] It has been noted that no playwrights gave tribute to Shakespeare for the 1623 Folio, save for Ben Jonson, whose assessment becomes the locus classicus for Shakespeare's scant knowledge of Greek and Latin in a poem that showcases Jonson's own mastery of the ancients. These early putdowns dog Shakespeare's reputation into the eighteenth century. As Schoenbaum has observed, "All these early memorialists dwell on the limitations of Shakespeare's learning."[66] Here follows a sampling: Thomas Fuller, "Indeed his Learning was very little";[67] Edward Phillips, "probably [Shakespeare's] Learning was not extraordinary."[68] Aubrey in his *Brief Lives* is rather more generous, allowing that Shakespeare "understood Latine pretty well," at least well enough to teach it (albeit in the provinces), as "a Schoolmaster in the Countrey."[69] For Rowe, Shakespeare's education stopped short of even the local grammar school curriculum. Financially strapped, his father "is forc'd to withdraw [his eldest son] from thence," and thereafter his learning was restricted to his father's wool-dealing trade (10). Rowe estimates that Shakespeare's knowledge of Latin was "about that of one of the *Gothick* princes" in *Titus Andronicus*, a reference to the loutish Chiron's recognition of a verse from Horace, familiar to Elizabethan schoolboys from its quotation, twice, in Lily's Latin grammar:[70] "which, I suppose, was the Author's Case" (iv).

One of the seventeenth-century anecdotes, perhaps the cruelest, grants Shakespeare even less than schoolboy Latin. As godfather to Ben Jonson's son, he gives him as his christening present "a dozen good latten spoons." These would have been christening spoons made not of silver, as was customary, but of "latten," a cheap copper alloy, but also the tongue in which they would have been inscribed. Shakespeare, as the story goes, must turn to Jonson to translate the inscriptions, though the mottos were typically in schoolboy Latin, on the order of *Fides* or *Deo Gratias*.[71] Once again, the anecdote assumes Shakespeare's limited country education at a time when the university was deemed the only gateway to the knowledge of the ancients and their languages expected of poets. Jonson was a rarity and even he was rumored by Thomas Fuller to have been "statutably admitted into st. Johns college in Cambridge," where he would have flourished had he not been summoned home to assist his bricklayer stepfather.[72]

In this context, it is tempting to reconsider Shakespeare's effigy on his Stratford funeral monument (Fig. 1.1). In his unpublished treatise on clothing and appearance, *Chronologia Vestiaria*, John Aubrey, having seen the monument perhaps as early as 1640, identifies the effigy's garment with the robes of his own alma mater:

> Mr William Shakespeare [Poet] in his monument in the Church at Stratford upon Avon, his figure is thus, viz a Tawny satten doublet I thinke pinked and over that a black gowne like an Under-gratuates at Oxford, scilicet the sleeves of the gowne doe not cover the armes, but hang loose behind.[73]

The art historian Nikolaus Pevsner, in his survey of funeral monuments in the Warwickshire area, accords the robes a higher academic status: "the iconographical type chosen is that of the scholar or divine."[74] In her recent biography of Shakespeare, Lena Cowen Orlin goes further still by focusing on a feature not mentioned by Aubrey or Pevsner: the cushion at the base of Shakespeare's effigy, supporting his quill-holding hand. This feature, too, has an Oxford provenance: she locates several early seventeenth-century "cushioned funerary monuments" of men renowned for their learning. For Orlin, not only does Shakespeare's monument conform to "the Oxford mould": it also may have been designed by Shakespeare himself, who must have been familiar with the style, she infers, from his frequent journeys through the university town between Stratford and London. If so, as she proposes in the arresting final sentence of her biography, "Shakespeare's last intentional act may have been to show us both how he looked in his own time and how he wanted to look for all time."[75] The irony is inescapable: the monument's iconography commemorates Shakespeare for the learning he in his own time and long thereafter was reputed to have notoriously lacked.

***

The legendary inadequacy of Shakespeare's education posed a particular challenge to his eighteenth-century publisher. Jacob Tonson, in collaboration with Cambridge University Press, was in the process of building an English literary canon comparable to that of the ancients. His strategy was to heighten the prestige of vernacular poets like Abraham Cowley, William Congreve, Beaumont and Fletcher, Milton, and Thomas Otway by publishing them in the same bibliographic format he had conferred on Horace, Virgil, Terence, and Catullus.[76] Each author was to be published in multi-volume sets with frontispiece, a textual apparatus, and a prefatory Life. A Life at the edition's threshold was not, then, Rowe's idea. Indeed, he begins his *Account* with a bemused apology for its presence. A Life, he explains, might satisfy a general curiosity about its subject, "[h]ow trifling soever this curiosity may seem to be." Or it might "sometimes conduce to the better understanding of his book," though Shakespeare's works "may seem to many not to want a Comment" (ii). But from the publisher's point of view, the packaging of Shakespeare as an ancient conferred the same kind of prestige as comparisons to the ancients did in Francis Meres's 1598 survey, *A Comparative Discourse of our English poets, with the Greeke, Latine, and Italian Poets.*[77] As Samuel Johnson recognized in the preface to his 1765 edition of Shakespeare, Rowe's edition was undertaken "that our authour's works might appear like those of his fraternity, with the appendages of a life and recommendatory preface."[78] In one problematic sense, however, as we have noted, Shakespeare was decidedly *not* of their fraternity.

How could a writer thought to have scant knowledge of the ancients possibly be raised to their literary level? The strain of the project is evident in the engraving reproduced as the frontispiece of all six volumes of Rowe's 1709 edition (Fig. 1.5).

Shakespeare is being crowned by Comedy and Tragedy, with winged Fame aloft, trumpeting his glory. The classicizing intent of the image is unmistakable: voluminously draped figures, laurel wreaths and branches, thespian masks and instruments, a raised plinth, and an arched recess of Corinthian pilasters. In a witty inversion, the classical world (with all its trappings) is paying homage to the modern author, in period doublet with loose shirt ties. Even the medium of his likeness is modern, a painted portrait, copied from the seventeenth-century Chandos portrait, in a newly fashionable oval frame.

Fig. 1.5 Shakespeare as classic by Michael van der Gucht,
frontispiece to all six volumes of Nicholas Rowe's edition of
Shakespeare (1709). © Bodleian Libraries, University of Oxford.

Yet certain incongruities are hard to conceal. Because Shakespeare, by the Folio's canonization, wrote in three genres, the histories must go unrepresented. And even the crowning of the other two is not quite deserved, as a reader would ascertain from Rowe's opinion that Shakespeare's plays are generally too mixed to be properly classified as either. Rowe considers only three plays pure comedy: *The Merry Wives of Windsor, The Comedy of Errors,* and *The Taming of the Shrew.* "The rest," he maintains, "however they are call'd, have something of both kinds" (xvii). The plays classified as tragedy are also hybrids, "inclind the way of Trage-comedy rather than exact Tragedy." That hapless dark Ignorance should in the engraving lie vanquished beneath Tragedy's right foot might also jar viewers accustomed to hearing Shakespeare's education disparaged.

It is no wonder that there are incongruities; the classicizing surrounds had been engraved for another author: Pierre Corneille (Fig. 1.6).[79] The honorific statuary is perfectly appropriate to the acclaimed neo-classical French dramatist, well versed in both the ancient authorities and their Italian redactions, author of the classical tetralogy of *Le Cid, Horace, Cinna,* and *Polyeucte.* Certainly, Corneille's marble bust sits more securely on the stone plinth than Shakespeare's modern oil portrait, which leans awkwardly and precariously on Tragedy's elongated left forearm. The Latin tag on Corneille's plinth—AMENT SERIQUE NEPOTES, "May he be praised by his descendants and posterity"—has been replaced by the familiar tag, "ob: A:D 1616. Aet: 53."

This engraving's embarrassments nicely illustrate the challenge of celebrating as a classic the poet renowned for his unfamiliarity with the classics. The best the defenders of his literacy can do is insist, as does Charles Gildon, "that *Shakespear* was not entirely ignorant of the Ancients"; all the same, Gildon adds, he would have been a better playwright still "had his Ignorance of them been much less, than it really was."[80] Toward the end of the century, the problem remains, even after Richard Farmer demonstrates that Shakespeare knew the classics, not in the original Greek and Latin, but through mediating translations and redactions. In Thomas Warton's three-volume *The History of English Poetry* (1781), considered England's first modern literary history, Shakespeare's extravagance remains salient: "We behold him breaking the

Fig. 1.6 Corneille as classic by Guillaume Vallet after Antoine Paillet, frontispiece to *Le Théâtre de P. Corneille* (1664). © Bridgeman Images.

barriers of imaginary method."[81] In 1783 the critic Hugh Blair, while acknowledging the greatness of Shakespeare's natural genius, admits "it is a genius shooting wild, deficient in just taste, and altogether unassisted by knowledge or art."[82]

***

Yet the problem proved productive. If Shakespeare was to be canonized as the preeminent English author, the discipline he lacked would have to be provided by others. In the first commentary to discuss the plays and the poems individually, Charles Gildon applies his redacted Aristotelean rules to Shakespeare's irregularities, making what for him is both a moral and aesthetic distinction between what is to be admired and what is to be blamed. He prefixes his "Remarks on the Plays of Shakespeare" with an essay in which he intends to "lay down such Rules of Art that the Reader may be able to distinguish [Shakespeare's] *Errors* from his *Perfections*". His main concern is that Shakespeare's failings not be mistaken for virtues so that readers "be drawn into an Erroneous Imitation of his Faults." Indeed, he reproves Rowe for having done just that when he allowed himself to entertain the possibility that the classical strictures might have detracted from the "beautiful Extravagance, which we admire in *Shakespear*." As we have seen, for Gildon, that is a logical impossibility, for "all that is pleases according to the Rules, and all that disgusts or is insipid, wild, or extravagant [is] contrary to them."[83]

For Pope, because Shakespeare's "great defects" almost matched his "great excellencies," he was the perfect subject for cultivating literary judgment or taste: "as he has certainly written better, so he has perhaps written worse, than any other." In Shakespeare's own time, according to Pope, "there was no establish'd judge, so every one took the liberty to write according to the dictates of his own fancy."[84] Nor were there critics, Johnson maintained, "of such authority as might restrain his extravagance."[85] Editors addressed Shakespeare's irregularity, aiming to rectify or perfect Shakespeare's text by evening out his meter, distinguishing prose from verse, dividing acts into scenes, and emending or elucidating obscure passages.

After the reopening of the theatres in 1660, dramatists, too, were keen to regularize his plays, to make them answerable to the unities, probability, and decorum as well as to modern refinements of syntax and meter. Dryden granted that Shakespeare was as worthy of modern veneration as Aeschylus was among the Greeks, but only if his plays were "alter'd" as he had altered *Troilus and Cressida,* "a heap of Rubbish" before it went through the refinements of his adaptation.[86] Nahum Tate's simile was more charitable, likening Shakespeare's *King Lear* to "a Heap of Jewels ... dazling in their Disorder" until he found the means "to rectifie what was wanting in the Regularity and Probability of the Tale" in his own notoriously successful adaptation of 1681.[87]

Thus, eighteenth-century criticism, editing, and performance all attempt to address the problem of Shakespeare's extravagance, the stylistic vagaries exemplified also in his fabled behavior, when knowledge of ancient writing and language was fundamental to poetic achievement. This will change, of course, in the next century, among idealists in Germany and those who read them in England, particularly Coleridge. In his lectures on Shakespeare, Coleridge summarizes the long-standing consensus that Shakespeare lacked knowledge: "In nine places out of ten in which I find his awful name mentioned, it is with some epithet of 'wild,' 'irregular,' 'pure child of nature,' &c."[88] And he credits himself with having turned the tide: "I own I am proud that I was the first in time who publicly demonstrated to the full extent of the position, that the supposed irregularity and extravagances of Shakespeare were the mere dreams of a pedantry."[89] For to Coleridge, these irregularities applied only to incidentals: "in all the essentials of art ... the Plays of Shakespeare were incomparably more coincident with the principles of Aristotle, than the productions of Corneille and Racine, notwithstanding the boasted regularity of the latter."[90] The notorious breaker of classical rules has become their true adherent. Wordsworth maintained the same:

[A]mong us it is a current, I might say, an established opinion, that Shakespeare is justly praised when he is pronounced to be "a wild irregular genius, in whom great faults are compensated by great beauties." How long may it be before this misconception passes away, and it becomes universally acknowledged that the judgement of Shakespeare in the selection of his materials and in the manner in which he has made them, heterogenous as they often are, constitute a unity of their own, and contribute to one great end?[91]

Within a few decades, the earlier critique of Shakespeare had been repudiated, as is clear in the memoirs of Charles Knight, the popular nineteenth-century editor and publisher of Shakespeare:

> We believe the time is passed when it can afford any satisfaction to an Englishman to hear the greatest of our poets perpetually held up to ridicule as a sort of inspired barbarian, who worked without method, and wholly without learning...the popular mind must be led in an opposite direction; and we must all learn to regard him as he really was, as the most consummate of artists, who had a complete and absolute control over all the materials and instruments of his art,...with entire self-possession and perfect knowledge.[92]

So Shakespeare by the middle of the nineteenth century has undergone a complete reappraisal: from "inspired barbarian" to "the most consummate of artists." No longer is knowledge of the ancient tongues and writings indispensable to literary pursuits—nor is the acquisition of that knowledge exclusive to university attendance. The anecdotes of transgression that circulated about Shakespeare into the eighteenth century cease to capture what was once perceived as the impropriety of Shakespeare's writing and behavior, his moral and stylistic deviance, both once seen to issue from the awkward fact of his limited formal education. The "traditional stories" lose their validity as literary criticism and are either dismissed as factually inaccurate or scrutinized for some fictionalized kernel of truth.

The reception of Shakespeare's work also changes. New imperatives come to direct criticism, editing, and staging. Criticism is not the application of rules to Shakespeare's vagaries but rather the tracking of the development of his singular genius by its own self-determining criteria. So, too, editing does not aim to "correct" or "perfect" a corrupt text but to recover what Shakespeare had put to paper. Plays are edited not as rewritten to conform with a later neoclassical aesthetic but instead with fidelity to his quarto and Folio texts. To accommodate this newly transvalued Shakespeare, a different kind of Life emerges: one that tracks (and marvels at) Shakespeare's development, from his rustic beginnings to his dramatic and poetic supremacy. To narrate that trajectory, something altogether novel has to be devised: a chronological continuum to connect the two endpoints of his birthdate and death date: the long dash between 1564 and 1616.

2

Shakespeare's Lifeline

As Shakespeare's Life had no dated endpoints until the eighteenth century, so too did it lack a chronological continuum connecting his birthdate to his deathdate. In what I have termed the biographical formula (1564–1616), that dated continuum is symbolized by the horizontal bar, the long dash, between the two termini. The continuum threads through the dated events of his life that are documented, like baptisms, burials, or mortgage deeds and loans. But it also runs through the dates when Shakespeare is ascertained to have written his works.[1] Once those dates are aligned, the narrative of the biography (1564–1616) need only follow the lead of the integrated chronological sequence.

Yet the chronology of Shakespeare's plays is late to be devised: for some two hundred years, the plays were encountered with little or no concern for when in his lifetime Shakespeare wrote them. As we saw, the first comprehensive collection of his works gave only two dates, 1616 and 1623, the date of Shakespeare's death and the date of the publication of his plays. When collected in that volume, the plays were grouped by dramatic genre rather than ranked in the chronological order that in the middle of the twentieth century became standard. Yet as the biography (1564–1616) replaces the uncalendared anecdotes, so the chronology of the plays phases out genre: critical attention shifts from the rules of ancient tradition to the development of Shakespeare's genius. Genres do resurface at the turn of the twentieth century, but only after they have been converted to stages of Shakespeare's life— early comedies, middle tragedies, late tragedies, and last romances—so that Shakespeare's plays, whether in generic groupings or chronological succession, can be seen to reveal the trajectory of his development.

***

There is a precedent for taking the rectilinear dash of the biographical formula as a representation of the continuum between cradle and grave. Only a few millimeters longer than the typographic em dash, it represents the duration of Shakespeare's lifetime:

It is one of two thousand lines etched on *A Chart of Biography*, a broadsheet measuring two feet by three feet, devised by the polymath Joseph Priestley and published in 1765. (For an impressionistic reduction of the broadsheet, see Fig. 2.1.)

Each line represents the life of one of the "most distinguished [persons] in the annals of fame" over a three-thousand-year expanse.[2] A "dated timeline" runs along both the top and the bottom of the chart, measuring in decades and centuries what Priestley calls "universal time," from 1200 BC to 1800 AD, with a cruciform fleur de lys marking the incarnational break between BC and AD time. With a ruler in hand, a viewer could align the two endpoints of any lifeline with the dated gradients at the top or bottom of the chart and thus determine the same details registered by the *DNB*'s biographical formula: the birthdate, the deathdate, and the span between them.

Each of the chart's two thousand lines, like Shakespeare's, forms a literal lifeline, or *bio-graph*, a graph of a life, at a time when the Greek cognate "biography" was settling into the English lexicon as a synonym for the Anglo-Saxon "life." When there is uncertainty about either endpoint (almost invariably it is the birthdate), the line breaks into dots, as is the case for two of the lifelines just before Shakespeare's (those of the poet Spenser and the versifier of the psalms, Thomas Sternhold):

In the right margin of the chart, the two thousand eminent lifelines have been divided into six bands of distinction: (1) Historians, Antiquarians, and Lawyers, (2) Orators and Critics, (3) Artists and Poets, (4) Mathematicians and Physicians, (5) Divines and Metaphysicians, and (6) Statesmen and Warriors. The chart's layout makes it possible to identify an eminent person's contemporaries in the various fields by glancing at the lifelines in the boxes directly above or below his or her

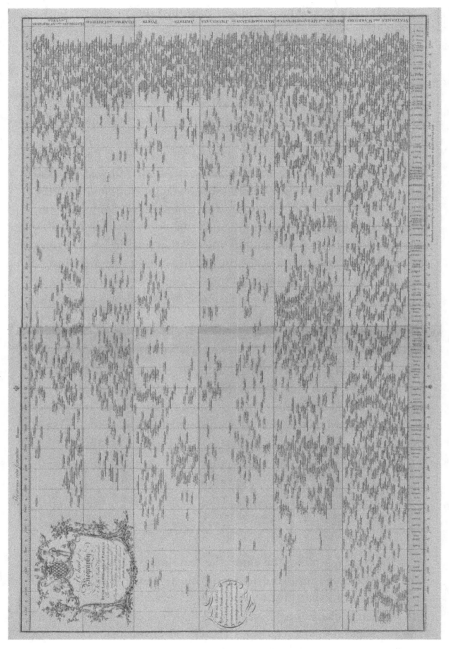

Fig. 2.1 *A Chart of Biography* with 2000 lifelines by Joseph Priestley, engraved broadsheet, 2′×3′ (1765). © Library Company of Philadelphia.

name. Among the scores of Shakespeare's contemporaries in each band, mainly but not exclusively English, are Coke (1), Casaubon (2), de Vega (3), Kepler (4), Grotius (5), and Shah Abbas (6). Also ascertainable is the eminent person's place in world historical time. At the bottom of the chart, just above the measured scale, the rulers of the world historical kingdoms are given, so the viewer can follow the progress of the *trans-latio imperii* schema as it moves from east to west, beginning with the four ancient empires: Assyrian, Persian, Hellenic, and Roman, the latter followed by its eastern remnant Byzantium. From the last of the Byzantine emperors (Constantine XI), the imperial mantle passes directly to William the Conqueror, followed by the succession of English sovereigns up to George II, the monarch preceding the chart's completion.

In the upper left corner, a motto gives the metaphor for the chart's direction: *Fluminis ritu feruntur*. These are Horace's words to Maecenas, urging him to stand fast while the world sweeps by like a river.[3] As Priestley notes in the pamphlet intended to accompany the chart, "Time is continually suggested to us, by the view of this chart, under the idea of a *river*, flowing uniformly on." The chart's two thousand lives, however eminent, are little more than "so many small straws swimming on the surface," the whole rectilinear convoy impelled forward from left to right as if by an inexorable current. Yet there is purpose to the flow, as is illustrated by the demographics of the chart. Though the population of warriors and statesmen remains dense throughout the course of time ("The world hath never wanted competitors for empire and power," Priestley notes in the pamphlet), the "crowds of names in the divisions appropriated to the arts and sciences" has doubled a hundredfold over the two centuries leading up to the present of the chart's devising. This bodes well for the future, especially for science, "advancing as it now does."[4] A few inches at the chart's right margin are left blank to allow its owners to inscribe the names of the meritorious whose lives are not yet complete—like Voltaire, Priestley suggests, who was still alive at the time of the chart's devising. After the year 1800, the last date on the chart's "universal time scale," a new broadsheet would need to be affixed in the same format and Priestley expresses regret that he himself will not live to see those rising illuminati. He could quite reasonably have expected his own lifeline (1733–1804) to appear among them.

Lives and lines have long shared an affinity. In palmistry, a line swerving from the base of the thumb across the palm indicates a life's future course; in mythology, the thread of life is wound on a spool before being measured out and cut; in genealogy, lines of descent extend on sprawling branches and sometimes splayed roots. But in *A Chart of Biography*, the line is straight and advancing, always from left to right. According to a recent study of the graphic representations of world historical time, the timelines on this 1765 chart are the first to be printed in England.[5] The technique is not innovative: engraved lines are perfectly familiar, on map grids, for example, or calendrical tables. It is the concept that is new. Priestley credits it to Isaac Newton, calling his own chart "a kind of ocular demonstration" of Newton's "most rational system" that imagines the passage of time as uniform and continuous. It is a novelty to represent not only lives but time itself (whether universal, biographical, or imperial) as an advancing straight line. The pamphlet explains the idea behind the chart's "mechanical contrivance": "the abstract idea of TIME ... admits of a natural and easy representation in our minds by the idea of a measurable space, and particularly that of a LINE; which, like time, may be extended in length."[6] On *A Chart of Biography*, duration in time is proportional to extension in space. Years, decades, and centuries are converted to millimeters.

Priestley's chart is an extraordinary feat of compression, abstraction, and calibration, and he takes pride in its having been achieved "without the intervention of words." Indeed, he regrets the necessity of having had to clutter the chart with surnames. Ideally, for him, a line's length and placement would suffice to identify its subject and thereby constitute a pure biometric. The *Dictionary of National Biography*, it might be said, does just the reverse: it converts the abstract line of the biograph into a chronologically driven biographical narrative.

***

In the first Life to preface Shakespeare's works, Nicholas Rowe's 1709 *Some Account*, there is no sign of Priestley's "abstract idea of TIME." As Chapter 1 maintained, the undated incidents comprising the account are episodic rather than continuous, self-contained rather than part of an extended and coherent whole. But Priestley's abstraction is very much on the mind of Edmond Malone, the author of the second prefatory Life of Shakespeare.[7] Indeed, the rectilinear might be seen as the regulating impulse behind his many scholarly projects. As his friend and literary executor James Boswell, Jr. observed in his memoir of him, "When sitting down to the perusal of any work, either ancient or modern, Malone's attention was drawn to its chronology."[8] His career abounds in examples. When advising James Boswell, Sr. on how to proceed with his biography of Samuel Johnson, Malone urged him to avoid the example of his subject, who "was generally careless of dates," and instead follow his own method: "Make a skeleton with references to the materials, in order of time."[9] Boswell complied: his *Life of Johnson* proceeds, as he acknowledges, "in the chronological series of Johnson's life, which I trace as distinctly as I can, year by year."[10] For the last twenty years of Johnson's life, Boswell had the great advantage of having Johnson's diary, but by his own account, that was not enough: "I have sometimes been obliged to run half over London, in order to fix a date correctly."[11]

Malone made such chronological skeletons for his own projected edition of Alexander Pope (never published) as well as of John Aubrey (also never published).[12] His first biographical essay, a brief memoir prefixed to the 1780 edition of Oliver Goldsmith's poems and plays, proceeds in dated sequence.[13] His *The Life and Writings of John Dryden* begins by discrediting previous accounts, including that of Johnson, who, according to Malone, was disinclined to examine "ancient registers, offices of record and those sepulchers of literature, publick repositories of manuscripts" and therefore had to rely on his memory for dates.[14] In the volumes of Dryden's plays edited by Malone, he attends to the chronological order of their writing, refining and tabulating the chronology of plays furnished by Dryden himself.[15] For this edition of Joshua Reynolds, he had in his possession all of his close friend's papers and was able to track not only the progress of his life, but also his steadily rising reputation, as reflected in the increasing prices commanded by his paintings.[16]

The subjects of his biographies and editions—Pope, Aubrey, Dryden, and Goldsmith—have their biometrical counterparts on Priestley's chart. Malone (1741–1812) may have known Priestley (1733–1804), for they shared several acquaintances, including Edmund Burke, Samuel

Johnson, and Edward Gibbon. He certainly knew Priestley's chart. The "Sale Catalogue of the Library of the Late Edmond Malone" (1818) includes editions of both Priestley's *A Chart of Biography* and his pamphlet *A Description of a Chart of Biography* discussing its use. Perhaps the chart was on display in Malone's library, giving graphic inspiration to his scholarly and literary pursuits.

The rectilinear also drives Malone's two most innovative Shakespeare projects: the chronologizing of the plays and the narrativizing of his life. The first resulted in an essay, "An Attempt to Ascertain the Order in which the Plays Attributed to Shakspeare were Written." First published in 1778 and revised at least three times (1785, 1790, 1821), it consisted of a numbered chronological table of the plays (Fig. 2.2), followed by an entry for each play of up to five pages explaining how each date had been determined.[17]

The second project, his *Life of Shakspeare,* was not published until after his death in 1812, though he worked on it intermittently for decades. When first proposing the Life in 1796, he advertised it as "a more regular life of our poet"—that is, one in which the materials he had amassed would be regulated by chronology, in seriatim.

Both projects, like Priestley's linear abstractions, were novel. Editors and critics had previously speculated on which play might have been Shakespeare's earliest, but no systematic attempt had been made to assign dates to the thirty-six Folio plays. Edward Capell had devised for the plays a "SCHEME of their succession" to accompany his edition, but ranked them in the order not of composition but of publication, "the dates of the earliest impressions."[18] Malone's *Life of Shakspeare,* too, was unprecedented. Rowe's anecdotal *Some Account of the Life, & c.* (1709) bore scant resemblance to what Malone had proposed: "an entirely new life of Shakespeare ... (compiled from original and authentic documents)."[19] The only documentary source consulted for Rowe's Life was the parish register; the rest was based on what Malone termed "traditional stories," passed from one generation to the next, "being frequently either wholly unfounded, or blended with the grossest fiction."[20]

The two epigraphs to all versions of the essay on chronology acknowledge the difficulty, indeed impossibility, of the task Malone set himself. In the first, from Statius's *Thebaid,* Amphion perceives an uncertain

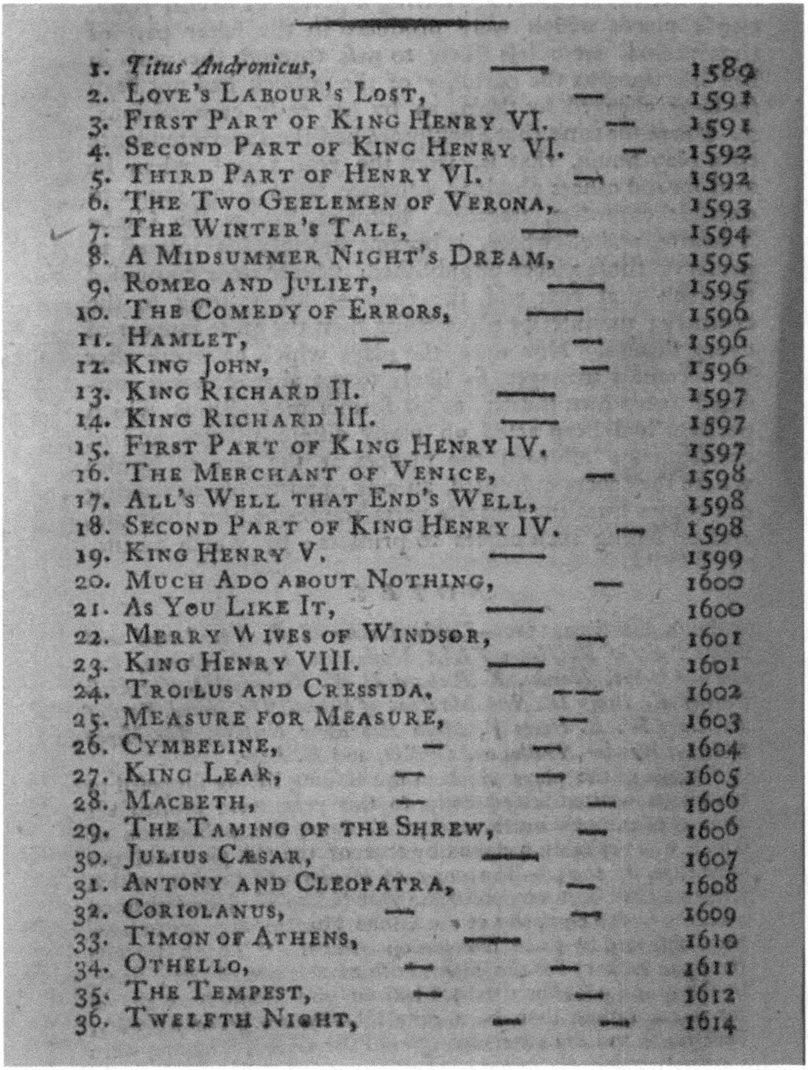

1. *Titus Andronicus*, —— 1589
2. Love's Labour's Lost, — 1591
3. First Part of King Henry VI. — 1591
4. Second Part of King Henry VI. — 1592
5. Third Part of Henry VI. — 1592
6. The Two Geelemen of Verona, 1593
7. The Winter's Tale, —— 1594
8. A Midsummer Night's Dream, 1595
9. Romeo and Juliet, —— 1595
10. The Comedy of Errors, —— 1596
11. Hamlet, — — 1596
12. King John, — — 1596
13. King Richard II. —— 1597
14. King Richard III. —— 1597
15. First Part of King Henry IV. 1597
16. The Merchant of Venice, — 1598
17. All's Well that End's Well, 1598
18. Second Part of King Henry IV. — 1598
19. King Henry V. —— 1599
20. Much Ado about Nothing, — 1600
21. As You Like It, —— 1600
22. Merry Wives of Windsor, — 1601
23. King Henry VIII. —— 1601
24. Troilus and Cressida. —— 1602
25. Measure for Measure, — 1603
26. Cymbeline, — — 1604
27. King Lear, — — 1605
28. Macbeth, — — 1606
29. The Taming of the Shrew, — 1606
30. Julius Cæsar, —— 1607
31. Antony and Cleopatra, — 1608
32. Coriolanus, — — 1609
33. Timon of Athens, —— 1610
34. Othello, — — 1611
35. The Tempest, — — 1612
36. Twelfth Night, — — 1614

Fig. 2.2 The plays in chronological order as ascertained by Edmond Malone, in *The Plays of William Shakspeare*, ed. Samuel Johnson, George Steevens, and Isaac Reed, 10 vols. (1785), I, 288.

motion, "dubium incertumque moveri" (X, 389–92); in the second, from Dante's *Purgatory*, the shade of Statius attempts to embrace the shade of Virgil, "come cosa salda" (II, 288). There was (and still is) no record of when Shakespeare wrote his first and last plays; it is assumed that those termini coincide with the dates of his first arrival in London and his last departure from there, but even if that were the case, there is no record of either. Not only are there no endpoints for the timeline of his writing life; there are also no certain collinear points for any single play. Title pages give the date of publication and for eighteen of them that date is seven years after Shakespeare's death. The Stationers' Register records the date of a publisher's right to publish. The Master of the Revels' office-book tells when a play was approved for court performance. These dates connect the plays to the book trade, to the playhouse, or to the court. But Malone wants dates that would tether the plays to Shakespeare's life, and these can be had only if he brings them into existence.

Lacking external evidence of their composition, Malone scours the plays themselves for topical allusions, what he terms "notes of time" (II, 407): "Shakspeare is fond of alluding to events occurring at the time he wrote" (II.331). By Malone's dubious logic, if the time of those alluded events can be dated, so can the "time he wrote" the plays. Shakespeare's son died in 1596; *King John*, he opines, featuring Constance's "pathetick lamentations" for the death of her young son Arthur," was likely written in the same year (II, 353). But the time an event occurred, even if documented, is invariably elusive. In the final act of *Romeo and Juliet*, he notes a reference to the practice that fatally delayed Friar Lawrence, the sealing up of houses in which "infectious pestilence did reign," and concludes, "Shakspeare probably had himself seen this practiced in the plague which raged in London in 1593" (II.349). Yet when dating *Timon of Athens* by its multiple references to the plague, he notes that Shakespeare must have experienced several plagues during his writing life: "The great plagues of 1593 and 1603 must have made such an impression upon Shakspeare," he believes, yet perhaps it was "the more immediate recollection of the plague which raged in 1609" (II, 456). Even if the event can be precisely dated, can Shakespeare's knowledge of it be? The date of the Ottoman sultan's fratricidal succession is on record ("Feb. 1596"), but how can we know the date when Shakespeare, as Malone puts it, "had it in contemplation" in order to write, "Not Amurath an Amurath succeeds/ But Harry Harry" (II, 359)? The most datable topical allusion occurs in *Henry V* when the Chorus anticipates the return of the Earl of Essex from Ireland. Shakespeare, Malone maintains, must have written the play *after* Essex's departure from London in April 15, 1599, but *before* his return on September 28, 1599—unless, as Malone allows in passing, the passage is "a subsequent insertion" (II, 360), a possibility, it must be stressed, that might invalidate any one of his "notes on time."

At the conclusion of his essay on the "Order of Chronology," Malone acknowledges the provisionality of his novel project. He admits to "errors and deficiencies" that he hopes will be addressed by "deeper and more successful researches" (II, 467). By the time he died, he had reranked the plays at least three times; by 1821, four other critics had published alternative chronologies.[21] Yet however radical the repositioning of the individual plays, the abstract schema represented by the dated columnar table remains a fixture [Fig. 2.2], intimating what Malone sought: "the gradations by which [Shakespeare] rose from mediocrity to 'the summit of excellence', from artless and sometimes uninteresting dialogues, to those unparalleled compositions" (II, 290–1). As time progresses, so does the quality of his art. Early plays, written before 1600, fall short: "imperfect versification ... artless and desultory dialogue, the irregularity of the composition" (II, 327); "hastening too abruptly ... to the denouëment" (II, 318). With the later plays, however, Shakespeare's creative powers begin to soar so that Malone challenges anyone "to enumerate ... among the plays produced before 1600, compositions of equal merit" to the five plays he initially places at the end of his chronology: *Othello, King Lear, Macbeth, The Tempest*, and in last position, *Twelfth Night* (II.291). In his final posthumously published chronology (1821), *The Tempest* shifts to last place and is thereby raised to the "summit of excellence": "the genius of our great poet *gradually expanded itself*, till, like his own Ariel, it flamed amazement" (II, 468).

Malone's second rectilinearly motivated project was also novel, in both content and form. His *Life of Shakespeare* was not only the first to be made up of "original and authentick documents," as he maintained, but

also the first to attempt a sequential narrative. From the start, he imagined the biography would contrast with Rowe's piecemeal precedent:
"At some future time I hope to weave the whole into one uniform and
connected narrative."[22] Before undertaking to write his new Life, Malone
set about invalidating Rowe's old one.[23] In his 1790 edition, Malone
reproduces Rowe's *Some Account of the Life, & c.*, with critical notes so
copious that even in reduced print they often outsize the text itself. As he
reports, his inquiries "overturned, on very satisfactory evidence, almost
every tale that we have been taught to believe concerning this extraordinary man."[24] The posthumous 1821 edition reprints Rowe's Life but now
without Malone's notes, which, according to his co-editor Boswell, "were
written for the purpose of demolishing almost every statement which
[Rowe's account] contained" (I, xix). They have been put to use elsewhere, as Boswell explains: Malone had incorporated them into his own
"more extensive and correct" biography.

Malone does accept one of Rowe's anecdotes, though only after mod-
ification. It tells of the Earl of Southampton's aforementioned gift to
Shakespeare:

> Lord Southampton at one time, gave [Shakespeare] a thousand
> Pounds, to enable him to go through with a Purchase which he heard
> he had a mind to. A Bounty very great, and very rare at any time, and
> almost equal to that profuse Generosity the present Age has shewn to
> *French* dancers and *Italian* Eunuchs.[25]

Malone does not question that the exorbitant gift was given, for he finds
record of Southampton's patronage in Shakespeare's dedications to him
of both *Venus and Adonis* (1593) and *Lucrece* (1594). He also assumes
that Shakespeare actually purchased what "he had a mind to" with
Southampton's gift. But he can find no property among Shakespeare's
assets worth the bespoke sum of £1,000. The gift was given, the purchase
was made, but the "extravagantly exaggerated" sum is "totally unwor-
thy of credit," until Malone scales it down to a more plausible £100
(II, 478–9). As we have seen, however, the exaggeration is the point of
the anecdote, commensurate with what the notoriously profligate Shakespeare "had a mind to." Malone assumes it was real estate, but Rowe's

conversion of the lavish sum to what it would purchase in his own day suggests something more outré.

The documents Malone uses in "demolishing" Rowe's Life also serve to make up the new one. As he explains to a correspondent, once he has collected them, he need only interconnect them: the materials "must be woven together and brought into a connected narrative."[26] In theory, the narrative had only to follow the lineup of dates, like stepping stones between two points. The materials might be quite disparate— for example, Shakespeare's father's death in 1601, his purchase of land for £320 in 1602, his performance in Jonson's *Sejanus* in 1603, his purchase of Blackfriars Gatehouse in 1613, the enclosure dispute in 1614, the drafting of his will in 1616. However heterogenous, the events could be linked, if not causally or thematically, by nothing more than their dated succession.

Like his essay on the chronological order of the plays, Malone's biographical narrative has, or rather was intended to have, a forward thrust. Shakespeare's father's straightened circumstances require the playwright's departure from Stratford. Once in London, Shakespeare's life is one of "gradual attainments" of property and wealth. Malone sees "another and gratifying instance of prosperity" in his application for the renewal of his grant of arms: "finding himself now rising into consequence (which we shall hereafter see was the case) and having acquired some wealth, he wished to derive honours to himself and his posterity" (II, 41). Malone takes one of his own greatest finds, a letter in which a neighbor, Richard Quiney, asks for help in procuring a loan—still the only letter we have addressed to Shakespeare (dated October 25, 1598)—as evidence that Shakespeare was prosperous enough to give financial help to his friends (II, 484–5). Having left Stratford because of his father's "pecuniary difficulties," he is able upon his death there to leave his family "in a state of comparative affluence" (II, 484). Instead of the life of repeated offence registered in the anecdotes (from poaching to insolence to adultery to blasphemy), the biographical Shakespeare experiences a gradual rise from penury "to considerable wealth," from obscurity to the admiration of "all the most accomplished men" of the day (II, 487), including Spenser, as well as the "approbation and favour" of the Earl of Southampton and finally of two successive monarchs

(II, 480). Shakespeare's limited formal education is no longer a problem, for the knowledge that counts is that acquired not at university but through experience: "the means and gradations whereby he acquired that consummate knowledge of mankind" (II, 3).

Despite Malone's commitment to a "uniform and continued narrative," his biography frequently veers off course. His very first sentence sends him backtracking: "Before we proceed further, it may be proper to ascertain..." In this instance, it is the spelling of Shakespeare's name (II, 1). No sooner is his birth in 1564 announced than the narrative has to retreat in time again, to correct the record and establish that his father was not a butcher or dealer in wool but a glover who sold cured and whitened skins. And then again before continuing with his account —"it may not be improper before we proceed further"—this time to give a view of Stratford's history and constitution (II, 42). When Shakespeare is on the verge of leaving Stratford, the narrative is detained by a long digression on Anne Hathaway's genealogy. Before Shakespeare can begin his theatrical career, Malone spends almost a hundred pages attempting to establish Spenser's recognition of his fellow literary genius through deep inquiry into two covert allusions to him. Long stretches describe futile searches for material. Like the day of his birth discussed in Chapter 1, the record of Shakespeare's marriage eludes him, as do the key dates of when Shakespeare arrived in London or retired to Stratford, the two endpoints of his working life and his literary output.

At Malone's death, his biography remained unfinished and it fell to his friend and literary executor James Boswell, Jr. to complete it. Boswell found the manuscript "strangely defective," and for good reason: it omitted an account of the period during which Shakespeare had written his plays. The narrative broke off just as Shakespeare had arrived in London. From the notes and fragments Malone had left, Boswell was able to cobble together Shakespeare's retirement and death in Stratford. But for the intervening two decades or so of his professional life in London, there was nothing—"a chasm ... which I am unable to supply" (I, vii). The manuscript lacked the crucial stretch—from 1592 to 1614 by Malone's first chronological table, from 1592 to 1611 by his last—during which Shakespeare wrote the plays that qualified him as subject of such exhaustive biographical inquiry.

Boswell, however, comes up with a convenient solution. He fills the gap with an independent essay already at hand, Malone's final version of *An Attempt to Ascertain the Chronological Order*, now a hefty 180 pages. Boswell makes no attempt to conceal the stopgap insertion. In the list of the volume's contents, he titles the biography *Mr. Malone's Life of Shakspeare, comprehending an Essay on the Chronological Order of his Plays*. The essay remains discrete, with its own running title. Dated entries for each of the plays substitute for what Shakespeare did in those decades; documents are painstakingly sifted to arrive at dates of composition. After the final entry for *The Tempest* 1611, Malone's *Life* resumes up to Shakespeare's death, followed by discussions of his will, his portraits and bust, and his descendants, as well as an appendix of documents.

Boswell feared his expedient might not have met with his mentor's approval. Yet the long inset was perfectly in keeping with Malone's method: the dates of the plays filled in the missing segment of Shakespeare's chronologized life. While unreadable as a biographical narrative, Malone's *Life of Shakspeare* stands as a striking if ungainly demonstration of how "the abstract idea of TIME" imagined as a single calibrated advancing line allows the works to be integrated with the Life.

The timeline determines more than the sequence of the plays and the narrative of the Life. At his death, Malone left instructions "to publish Shakespeare's plays" in the order he supposed them to have been written. While never claiming certainty for his chronology, Malone had intended it to be fixed in the printing of his edition. By encountering the plays in the prescribed order of their writing, Malone assumed, readers would experience Shakespeare's creative development as they made their way through the numbered set of volumes:

[T]he reader might be thus enabled to trace the progress of the author's powers, from his first and imperfect essays, to those more finished performances which he afterwards produced. ... We shall now find his powers gradually developed as his knowledge became more extensive, and his judgment matured. (I, xvii)

The new arrangement was radical: it ousted the prevalent generic logic of the seventeenth-century folios and the eighteenth-century multi-volume editions.

Boswell was content to comply with Malone's instructions in the arrangement of the comedies and tragedies, what he loosely termed "the miscellaneous plays," but not "the dramas which were founded on English history." While endorsing the schema that would demonstrate Shakespeare "advancing in his progress to excellence," he questioned whether the order of royal succession should be superseded by that of authorial development, so that *Richard III*, for example, would precede *Richard II*. Finding the proposal "universally objected to by all whom I had an opportunity to consult" (I, xvii), Boswell was emboldened to deviate from his mentor's instruction. He drew additional support from the authority of Samuel Johnson, who believed that Shakespeare had intended most of the histories "to be read in regular connection," that is, in the order of English rule. The "historical chain" was thereby preserved (XV, 189). The ten histories in regnal order were sequestered to "a separate class" in volumes sixteen to nineteen. Instead of reproducing a uniform timeline demonstrating Shakespeare's artistic progress, the series was broken into two competing ones: the biographical and the regnal, one tracking Shakespeare's development and the other the succession of kings.

In his overview of Shakespeare biography, Samuel Schoenbaum assesses Malone's importance: "He had erected a new foundation for the study of Shakespeare's life."[27] In theory, this is certainly the case. Malone had the idea of a Life, 1564–1616, consisting of a dated continuum that runs through both what Shakespeare did and what he wrote. But as we have seen, the reality of his biography falls badly short. Crammed with a welter of documents assembled both to validate and invalidate materials often tangential to Shakespeare, it cannot hold to its notional chronological throughline. Unlike the idealized advancing timeline imagined behind Shakespeare's life and works, it has itself no momentum. Subsequent scholars used Malone's biography as a reference, but as a narrative it is impossibly mired in factual detail and speculation. Unlike Rowe's Life, it never circulated independently of the edition for which it was written.[28]

The biography Malone envisioned made up of "authentick documents" forming "one uniform and connected narrative" was standardized by Sidney Lee in his 500-page *A Life of William Shakespeare* (1898), an amplification of his *DNB* entry, reprinted thirteen times in his lifetime. The biography's ten-page table of contents itself demonstrates how a chronological throughline gives apparent coherence and direction to an otherwise scattered disarray of particulars. It includes dates, culled from documents but also from the chronology of the plays, for example: 1596–9 "The coat of arms," 1597 "The purchase of New Place," 1599 *Much Ado* and 1599 *As You Like It*, 1600 *Twelfth Night*, 1611 *The Tempest*, 1613 "Purchase of house in Blackfriars." Lee also contributed what in the twentieth century became the standard prefatory life to editions of Shakespeare's complete works.[29] His overview of that life draws on the same fluvial metaphor as Priestley's biograph: "the mighty stream of his potentiality, which is always moving onwards, always expanding, always deepening." The development of all authors, he suggests, follows that course, but none so forcibly as Shakespeare's: "No author's works offers clearer evidence than his of the steady and orderly growth of purely poetic faculty, of imagination and dramatic insight."

In the earlier anecdotal accounts, Shakespeare never changed: he was rude from start to finish, in his life but also in his work, his signature unruliness remedied only through the corrective redactions of editors, critics, and adapters. Under the auspices of the advancing timeline, however, irregularities reflect stages of his self-realization. His salient feature is his development, as his *DNB* biographer maintains: "in a survey of his complete achievement, the feature that overshadows all others is the steadiness with which his poetic, artistic, dramatic power marches forward to perfection."[30] Neither his life nor his works are blamed for what earlier centuries perceived as their undisciplined excess. As Malone's co-editor James Boswell, Jr. had confidently stated, "We may lament we know so little of his history but this, at least, may be asserted with confidence, that at no time was the slightest imputation cast upon his moral character" (XX, 220). Nor is either his biographical or his critical reputation marred by allegations of inadequate learning. Malone feels no need to defend or regret Shakespeare's "moderate knowledge of Latin," untroubled by what he regards as the likelihood that "he never attained such mastery of that language as to read it without the occasional aid of a dictionary" (II, 103–4). Indeed, not even that aid was necessary when, as Richard Farmer in his *An Essay on the Learning of Shakespeare* (1767) had demonstrated, to the satisfaction of Malone, the key texts of the ancients were readily available to Shakespeare—in translation.[31]

***

The volume that defined Shakespeare's dramatic canon, the 1623 Folio, provided only one date besides that of Shakespeare's death: 1623, the date of its publication. No dates are given for when Shakespeare wrote a play, for its organizing principle is genre, observed both in its title, *Mr. William Shakespeares Comedies, Histories & Tragedies*, and in the generic groupings of the catalogue page, each with its own quadrilateral niche and independent page signature sequences (Fig. 2.3).

Like its grand dimensions, the Folio's generic divisions were designed to lift Shakespeare's modern vernacular plays into the prestigious ranks of the ancient tradition that had defined the genres.[32] In his *A Comparative Discourse of our English poets with the Greeke, Latine, and Italian poets*, Francis Meres establishes the literary status of the English poets by relating them to the ancients. He pairs Shakespeare with the ancient poets who wrote in the same genres: with Ovid for his poems, with Plautus for his comedies, and with Seneca for his tragedies:

> [The] sweete wittie soule of *Ouid* liues in mellifluous & hony-tongued *Shakespeare*, witnes his *Venus* and Adonis, his *Lucrece*, his sugred Sonnets ... As *Plautus* and *Seneca* are accounted the best for Comedy and Tragedy among the Latines: so *Shakespeare* among the English is the most excellent in both kinds for the stage.[33]

That Shakespeare, unlike the ancient dramatists, wrote "in both kinds" is, for Meres, a particular distinction.

As we have seen, the first eighteenth-century edition of Shakespeare attempted to elevate him to the rank of a classic poet not only by publishing his plays in the bibliographic format identified with editions of the ancients but also by fronting each of its six volumes with the repurposed engraving of Shakespeare laureated by Tragedy and Comedy (Fig. 1.5). Shakespeare, notorious for his neglect of the ancients, did not fit comfortably in a frame designed for a neo-classical poet. Indeed there is no allegorical figure for one of the genres in which he wrote, at least after the 1623 Folio had wedged *Histories* between *Comedies* and *Tragedies*, both on its title page and in its catalogue. In canonizing Shakespeare's plays,

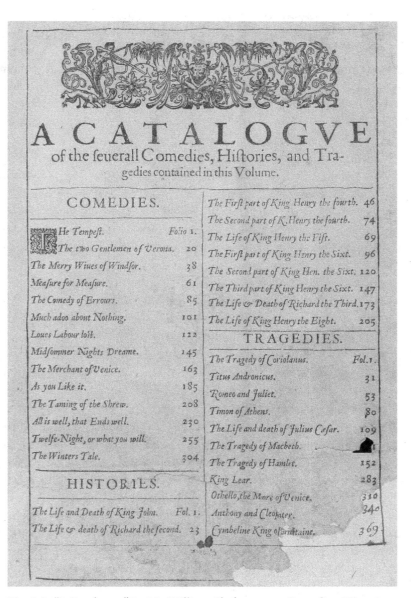

A CATALOGVE

of the feuerall Comedies, Hiſtories, and Tragedies contained in this Volume.

COMEDIES.

He Tempeſt.   Folio 1.
The two Gentlemen of Verona.   20
The Merry Wiues of Windſor.   38
Meaſure for Meaſure.   61
The Comedy of Errours.   85
Much adoo about Nothing.   101
Loues Labour loſt.   122
Midſommer Nights Dreame.   145
The Merchant of Venice.   163
As you Like it.   185
The Taming of the Shrew.   208
All is well, that Ends well.   230
Twelfe-Night, or what you will.   255
The Winters Tale.   304

HISTORIES.

The Life and Death of King Iohn.   Fol. 1.
The Life & death of Richard the ſecond. 23

The Firſt part of King Henry the fourth. 46
The Second part of K. Henry the fourth.   74
The Life of King Henry the Fift.   69
The Firſt part of King Henry the Sixt. 96
The Second part of King Hen. the Sixt. 120
The Third part of King Henry the Sixt. 147
The Life & Death of Richard the Third. 173
The Life of King Henry the Eight.   205

TRAGEDIES.

The Tragedy of Coriolanus.   Fol. 1.
Titus Andronicus.   31
Romeo and Juliet.   53
Timon of Athens.   80
The Life and death of Julius Cæſar. 109
The Tragedy of Macbeth.
The Tragedy of Hamlet.   152
King Lear.   283
Othello, the Moore of Venice.   310
Anthony and Cleopatr.   340
Cymbeline King of Britaine.   369

Fig. 2.3 "A Catalogue," in *Mr. William Shakespeares Comedies, Histories,
& Tragedies* (1623). © Bodleian Libraries, University of Oxford.

the Folio's boldest intervention was its introduction of a genre for which there was no classical dramatic precedent. It grouped together ten plays as a discrete unit linked together chronologically, in the order of regnal succession, from *King John* to *King Henry VIII*. Similar titles gave them additional coherence, indicating their common source in chronicle history. The titular prefix "Life and Death" as well as the division of two of the plays, *Henry IV* and *Henry VI*, into parts precluded any regard for the classical unities.

The three subsequent seventeenth-century folios (1632, 1663/4, 1685) follow the generic arrangement of the first. Even after the 1663 Folio appends seven plays to the original thirty-six, each of which had been associated in print with Shakespeare's name, the catalogue's generic groupings remain intact for the original thirty-six plays. By the time of the Fourth Folio (1685), however, their authority is clearly on the wane (Fig. 2.4).

The catalogue is relegated to the bottom half of the page, beneath the list of principal actors, by 1685 all long deceased; the font case has dropped from upper to lower; the self-containing frames have disappeared—as has one of the three generic headings, "Comedies."

When in 1709 the folio format splits into the multi-volumed octavos, the Folio's generic emphasis is retained, even heightened. In addition to the classicizing engraving (Fig. 1.5) each of the comedies·and tragedies is preceded by its own title page, with its genre printed larger and bolder than the play title itself. Some alterations are introduced in subsequent editions, in the interest of stressing and refining the generic distinctions. Alexander Pope gives two volumes of his elegant six-volume quarto edition of *The Works of Shakespeare* (1725) to each of the three folio genres. The comedies retain their Folio order, but *King Lear* is placed at the head of the histories, no doubt because, like all the histories of the English kings, it is sourced in Holinshed, as is indicated by the chronicle title Pope assigns it: *The Life and Death of King Lear*.[34] Attention to source also motivates Pope's greatest innovation: the division of the tragedies into two subgenres. Volume 5 contains "Tragedies from History" and volume 6 "Tragedies from Fable." The plays from "History" are drawn from the Roman historians, mainly Plutarch. Those from "Fable" are

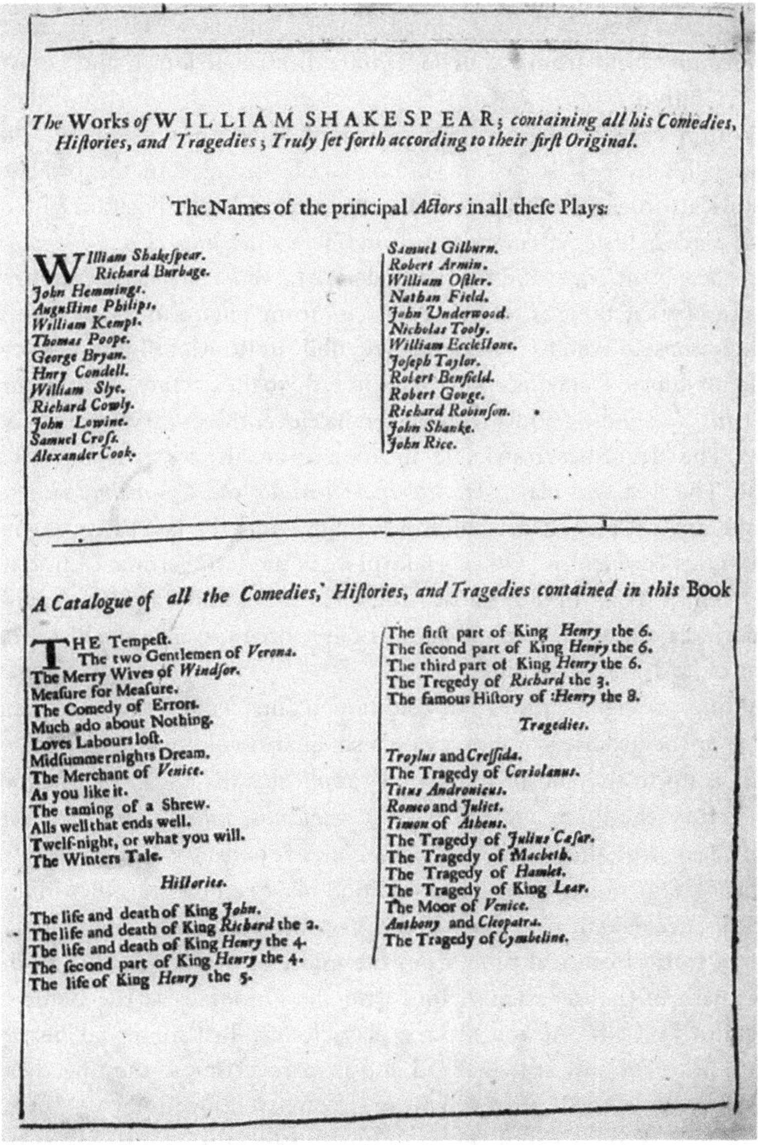

The Works *of* W I L L I A M S H A K E S P E A R; *containing all his Comedies, Histories, and Tragedies; Truly set forth according to their first Original.*

The Names of the principal *Actors* in all thefe Plays:

W *Illiam Shakespear.*
   Richard Burbage.
John Hemmings.
Augustine Philips.
William Kempt.
Thomas Poope.
George Bryan.
Hnry Condell.
William Slye.
Richard Cowly.
John Lowine.
Samuel Crofs.
Alexander Cook.

Samuel Gilburn.
Robert Armin.
William Ostler.
Nathan Field.
John Underwood.
Nicholas Tooly.
William Ecclestone.
Joseph Taylor.
Robert Benfield.
Robert Gouge.
Richard Robinfon.
John Shanke.
John Rice.

A Catalogue of all the Comedies, Histories, and Tragedies contained in this Book

T HE Tempeft.
   The two Gentlemen of *Verona.*
The Merry Wives of *Windfor.*
Meafure for Meafure.
The Comedy of Errors.
Much ado about Nothing.
Loves Labours loft.
Midfummernights Dream.
The Merchant of *Venice.*
As you like it.
The taming of a Shrew.
Alls wellthat ends well.
Twelf-night, or what you will.
The Winters Tale.

Histories.

The life and death of King *John.*
The life and death of King *Richard* the 2.
The life and death of King *Henry* the 4.
The fecond part of King *Henry* the 4.
The life of King *Henry* the 5.

The firft part of King *Henry* the 6.
The fecond part of King *Henry* the 6.
The third part of King *Henry* the 6.
The Tregedy of *Richard* the 3.
The famous Hiftory of *:Henry* the 8.

Tragedies.

Troylus and *Creffida.*
The Tragedy of *Coriolanus.*
Titus Andronicus.
Romeo and *Juliet.*
Timon of *Athens.*
The Tragedy of *Julius Cafar.*
The Tragedy of *Macbeth.*
The Tragedy of *Hamlet.*
The Tragedy of King *Lear.*
The Moor of *Venice.*
Anthony and *Cleopatra.*
The Tragedy of *Cymbeline.*

Fig. 2.4 "A Catalogue," in *Mr. William Shakespeares Comedies, Histories, & Tragedies* (1685). © Folger Shakespeare Library.

taken from modern novels or romances. In Pope's reductive schema, *Troilus and Cressida* derives from Chaucer, *Cymbeline* from Boccaccio, *Romeo and Juliet* from Bandello, *Hamlet* from Belleforest, and *Othello* from Cinthio.

Within each of these subgenres, another order is observed. The "Tragedies from History" in volume 5 are arranged in the order of historical time, determined not by Shakespeare's composition but by their place in history: *Timon of Athens, Coriolanus, Julius Caesar, Antony and Cleopatra, Titus,* and the anomalous *Macbeth.* The significant time is of a play's action, as set by its source—from Timon in the era of the Peloponnesian War, to Coriolanus's republican Rome, to Julius Caesar's dictatorship, to Octavius's imperial Rome, up to the decline of the empire in *Titus,* and ending oddly with Macbeth's eleventh-century rule in Scotland. The "Tragedies from Fable" in volume 6 are also sorted by historical time. The first two plays, *Troilus and Cressida* and *Cymbeline,* are set in the ancient past of Troy and of Britain, while the last three, *Romeo and Juliet, Hamlet,* and *Othello,* take place in modern Verona, Denmark, and Venice. Thus, in the case of both the histories and tragedies, a play's generic classification is an indication of its source as well as the historical time of its dramatic action.

While no eighteenth-century edition retains Pope's tragic subgenres (nor the generic symmetry of his six quarto volumes), every major edition up to the end of the century replicates his ancient and modern triads: the three ancient plays (*Coriolanus, Julius Caesar, Antony and Cleopatra*) and the three modern ones (*Romeo and Juliet, Hamlet, Othello*). One nineteenth-century edition places all the tragedies in historical succession, from *Troilus and Cressida* to *Othello,* the first and last in world historical time, from the midst of the Trojan War to the aftermath of the Venetian victory over the Ottomans at the Battle of Lepanto (1571).[35] As the history plays follow British regnal history (with *Macbeth* now at their head and *Lear* reverting to the tragedies), the tragedies observe universal history, from twelfth-century BC *Troilus and Cressida* to sixteenth-century *Othello.* With this dispensation, the plays make up two chronologies, neither pertaining to the time of Shakespeare's writing. Instead, both follow the represented dramatic action, as specified in the sources and in keeping with their generic assignment.

A generic consolidation of the atemporal comedies is also attempted. In several editions, including Samuel Johnson's, the comedies are arranged by place rather than time. The table of contents begins with *The Tempest* and *A Midsummer Night's Dream*, both set in magical surrounds. Then follows *The Merchant of Venice, Two Gentleman of Verona*, and *Measure for Measure* (set in Vienna); like city comedies, they are affiliated by their urban locales. By contrast, the remaining five comedies share pastoral or rural retreats: the forest of *As You Like It*, the park of *Love's Labour's Lost*, the Illyrian seacoast of *Twelfth Night*, the Bohemian countryside of *The Winter's Tale*, and the woodlands of *The Merry Wives of Windsor*.

As Samuel Johnson notes, the compilers of the Folio "seem not to have distinguished the three kinds, by any very exact or definite ideas."[36] Nicholas Rowe's 1709 edition had retained the Folio classification while querying its accuracy. The history plays, he maintained, as well as some of the comedies, "are really Tragedies." Only three of the comedies—*The Merry Wives of Windsor, The Comedy of Errors*, and *The Taming of the Shrew*—are "pure Comedy;" "the rest, however they are call'd, have something of both Kinds."[37] That Shakespeare's plays resisted the ancient genres or rules meant that editors and critics had to work all the harder to uphold their authority. Their adjustments allow for the emergence of new affinities across the generic divides. Pope's division of the tragedies into "Tragedies from History" and "Tragedies from Fable" invites linkages with both the histories and the comedies. Like the histories, "Tragedies from History" dramatize the historical record, Greco-Roman rather than English. Like the comedies, "Tragedies from Fable" derive from fictive novels and romances. The two triads (*Coriolanus, Julius Caesar, Antony and Cleopatra*; *Romeo and Juliet, Hamlet, Othello*) observe the division between the ancient and the modern.[38] However intended by the editor or publisher, these generic reshufflings are decidedly not motivated by any interest in when Shakespeare wrote the plays and how that order tracks his creative development.

The alterations to the Folio order, while introducing finer discriminations, still adhere to genre as the ordering principle. Shakespeare's plays must be generically tagged, however controversially, in order to qualify for critical discussion, for it is through the category of genre or literary kinds that they can be put into relation with the ancients and their vernacular successors. Nowhere is this more obvious than in the volume that was appended to Rowe's 1709 edition by Charles Gildon in 1710, containing Shakespeare's poems and two essays by Gildon. In the first essay, "On the Art, Rise and Progress of the Stage in Greece, Rome and England," Gildon explains the "particular Rules of the Stage as Aristotle has laid them down," discussing in full his definitions of tragedy and comedy, stressing in particular the unity of action and the necessity of probability.[39] In the second essay, "Critical Remarks on [Shakespeare's] Plays" Gildon applies those rules to each of Shakespeare's 1623 Folio plays as well as more briefly to his poems. His intention is clear: "I lay down such Rules of Art that the Reader may be able to distinguish [Shakespeare's] *Errors* from his *Perfections.*"

While maintaining that Shakespeare knew more of the ancients than Rowe had allowed—citing, for example, the two classically themed narrative poems, one with a Latin epigraph—Gildon grants that Shakespeare knew nothing about the rules of drama. If he had, Gildon maintains in his "Critical Remarks," "he wou'd have been the *Sophocles* of *England*, as he is now but little more, than the *Thespis* or at most the *Æschylus.*" Gildon analyses each of the Folio's thirty-six plays in the tripartite Folio order (also followed by Rowe's 1709 edition) in order to demonstrate "how far [Shakespeare] has succeeded by the Force of Nature, and where he has fail'd."[40] The failure of his natural powers is particularly notable in his handling of plots—for Aristotle, the most important part of a play. The tragedies suffer from irregular plotting, while the comedies are less affected because more dependent on character, for which Shakespeare, Gildon believes, had a natural bent. Unlike Rowe, who maintained that the histories were for the most part impure tragedies, Gildon defends them as a dramatic kind, "Draughts of the Lives of Princes brought into *Dialogue*," while admitting that their origin in the sprawling chronicles precludes any unity of plot. As he learned from Aristotle's criticism of poets who had written a *Theseid* or a *Heracleid*, emphasis on a single eponymous individual (Theseus or Hercules) cannot substitute for a unified plot (*Poetics,* I, viii). Furthermore, as with the comedies and tragedies, the histories have precedents among the ancients: in the "Greek Pieces, that were wrote before *Aeschylus* and *Sophocles* ... Or the rambling unartful Pieces first represented in *Rome* after the calling in of the *Etrurian* Players."[41] The generic status he grants the histories, he denies the tragicomedies. Their combination of "Grief and Laughter," two incompatible "Copies of Nature," is unnatural, "monstrous and shocking," and inimical to the law of kinds.[42]

In the final section of the essay, Gildon extends his critical remarks to Shakespeare's poetry, the two verse narratives and the collection entitled *His Miscellany Poems,* an edition of John Benson's 1640 *Poems* that, as Chapter 4 will discuss, includes most of Shakespeare's 1609 *Sonnets* in addition to verses by other poets. Here, too, a genre must be named and defined if a critical discussion is to proceed. Gildon names the forms he identifies within the miscellany—lyric, elegiac, and epigrammatic—and gives "an Abridgement of the Rules" for each poetic genre. Believing that most of the 1640 poems qualify as epigrams, he concentrates on that genre, with reference to Martial and Catullus: "How far Shakespear has excellid in this Way, is plain from his Poems before us."

In the Malone–Boswell edition of 1821, chronology replaces genre as both organizing rubric and critical focus. Yet in the succeeding decades, only one edition follows its radical supplanting of the Folio order. Charles Knight, in one of his many editions of Shakespeare, publishes the plays "according to the evidence of the dates of their composition," though here, too, the order is only partial.[43] Out of deference to the historical chain, he, like Boswell, exempts "the Chronology of the several Reigns." Soon after Malone, a number of scholars devise chronologies, among them Edward Capell, James Hurdis, Nathan Drake, and Alexander Chalmers, but the result is a reversion to the original unmodified 1623 Folio order. As one editor concluded, without any better alternative it was best to adhere to that old standby: "We could not do better than adopt the course pursued in 1623, so near to the time when Shakespeare was living."[44] The original Folio order thus resumes its primacy, observed by both the authoritative nine-volume Cambridge edition (1863–66) and its single volume compact derivative, the Globe edition (1864), intended for worldwide circulation. But while the order is retained, the once salient three generic titles and their typographic groupings have been dropped.

***

Without its generic rubrics, the original Folio arrangement comes to appear quite arbitrary. Toward the end of the nineteenth century, the founder of the Shakespeare Society, F. J. Furnivall, deemed the order "higgledy-piggledy, beginning with Shakspere's almost-last play, the *Tempest*, and then putting his (probably third), the *Two Gentlemen of Verona*, next it." With the works so scrambled, "No wonder readers are all in a maze."[45] Establishing the chronology—"the order of the maker's making"—was the "essential prerequisite" for observing "the growth of Shakspere's mind and art." The Society's mandate was urgent: "Do all you can to further the study of Shakspere, chronologically and as a whole, throughout the nation."

To the chagrin of the Society, another nation had already achieved this goal. In Germany, an edition in chronological order had been published, as well as a critical commentary discussing the works in that order.[46] Both were quickly translated and published in England. In their wake appeared Edward Dowden's *Shakspere: A Critical Study of His Mind and Art* (1875) and its distillation in the primer *Shakspere* (1878). Like the German editor and critic, and like his own fellow Irishman Edmond Malone, Dowden had no compunction about dismantling the order of the succession of English kings in order to bring Shakespeare's development into view. Finally the plays could be given a full chronological lineup without threatening the venerated "historical chain." Dowden's application of the "chronological method" leads to a remarkable result. He retrieves for Shakespeare's plays what, as we have seen, had become by the end of the nineteenth century an obsolete classification. He reinstates genre, but not as the traditional literary category by which Shakespeare's poetic status in relation to the ancients could be debated.

Genres are now phases or "periods" of Shakespeare's creative life. In both Dowden's Shakespeare primer and his critical study, Shakespeare's career begins in the realm of the outer and material, first "*In the work-shop*" of the comedies (1590 to 1595/6) before expanding "*In the world*" of the histories (1595/6 to 1600/1). At the turn of the century, it shifts to the higher realm of the inner or spiritual, so that Shakesepeare writes *"Out of the depths"* with the tragedies, (1601 to 1608), to arrive ultimately at his transcendent apogee, *"On the heights"* of the "last plays" (1608 to 1611 or 1613). In his first edition of *A Critical Study*, Dowden lacks a generic correlative for Shakesepeare's fourth phase. But in his Primer and all subsequent editions of *A Critical Study*, by bold critical fiat, he introduces one: "Let us, then, name this group, consisting of four plays, Romances." The correlation is now complete: each of the biological and psychological phases of Shakespeare's life—early, middle, late and last—have generic analogues, so that Shakespeare's complete corpus, dramatic and poetic, can be discussed in terms of development or growth, however at times uneven or sporadic. Genre, once presiding over the reproduction and discussion of Shakespeare's plays, is first displaced by chronology and later recuperated—but now converted from a category of criticism to stages of biography.[47]

Shakespeare's progression through the genres is unlike that of Virgil or Ovid, who attained literary preeminence by mastering a series of increasingly challenging and prestigious genres, from pastoral to georgic to epic. His development appears not programmatic but spontaneous. Inwardly impelled, his singular genius realizes itself uniquely in and through time. For the anecdotal Life, Shakespeare's rustic upbringing leaves him with a chronic lack of discipline, persisting through his lifetime, marking both his character and that of his writing, remediable only through the learned efforts of later editors, playwrights, and critics. By contrast, for the Life (1564–1616), the humbler his origin, the steeper and more impressive his ascent: from lowly beginnings to unsurpassable poetic supremacy. The biographical anecdotes exist by being retold and reprinted. But the biographical narrative requires more than tradition for its authorization. It needs an archive of materials, above all in Shakespeare's own hand: letters, diaries, notes, drafts of his playscripts. And herein lies the particular challenge of writing Shakespeare's biography: no such autograph papers exist. As Malone laments in his attempt to eke out a continuous biography based on authentic materials, "It is impossible not to express an unavailing regret that ... we are not in possession of a single manuscript from [his] pen..." (II.486).

3

Shakespeare's Archive

Edmond Malone collected more primary documents relating to Shakespeare than anyone before or since.[1] The records he discovered, transcribed, and reproduced form the foundation of the archive that is now readily accessible in both print and digital format.[2] Yet there is a great lacuna in his collection. Not only are there no manuscripts of Shakespeare's plays and poems;[3] as Malone lamented with "unavailing regret," except for a few signatures, there was no writing in his hand at all.[4]

For Malone, the blame for this dearth falls squarely on the successive generations between himself and Shakespeare. As a result of their indifference, the arduous task fell upon him to recover through what he terms his "biographical researches" the materials they should have preserved.[5] But there is another explanation. As Roger Chartier has observed, the authorial archive is a new phenomenon in the eighteenth century. Only then do authors begin to arrange for the survival not only of their works in print but also of all collateral handwritten materials. Rousseau and Goethe, Chartier's main examples, are among the first "archivists of themselves," assembling drafts, fragments, and notes—in their own hand.[6] While their contemporary Malone shared this desideratum, neither Shakespeare nor his immediate successors thought to set aside a store of autograph authorial papers. No wonder then that Malone's exhaustive searches proved disappointing to him. He was looking to recover a legacy that had never existed.

***

At the very start of his career as Shakespearean scholar, on a brief visit to London from Dublin, Edmond Malone accompanied George Steevens, the foremost Shakespearean editor of the day, to the Prerogative Office of the Doctors' Commons, where Shakespeare's original will had been filed, "in order to get a facsimile of the handwriting." Malone, as will be his routine, documents the occasion: "In the year 1776 Mr. Steevens, in my presence, traced with the utmost accuracy the three signatures affixed by the poet to his Will."[7] One can imagine the solemnity of the occasion: the first reproduction of Shakespeare's signature. Malone must have looked on intently as Steevens placed a translucent sheet of paper over each of the three signatures Shakespeare had written on the parchment just weeks before his death and traced "with utmost accuracy" every tremor of Shakespeare's palsied hand. The tracings were then given to an engraver to incise on a metal plate from which they were printed, first in the Johnson–Steevens' edition of 1778 (Fig. 3.1), and again in the Johnson–Steevens–Reed edition of 1785 and Malone's editions of 1790 and 1821.

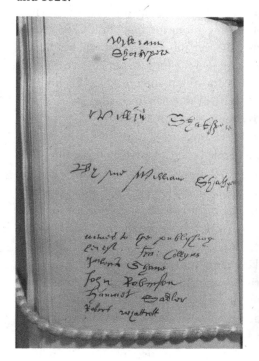

Fig. 3.1 The first facsimiles of the signatures on Shakespeare's will, in *The Plays of William Shakspeare*, ed. Samuel Johnson and George Steevens, 10 vols. (1778), I, after 200.

Owners of these editions might now have in their possession exact copies of Shakespeare's signature: their own specimens of what was then the only script from the hand that wrote the most revered plays and poems in the language.

In 1788, when Malone was preparing his own edition of Shakespeare, another steadier signature by Shakespeare came to light, this one written three years before his death, "in a fair good hand."[8] It, too, was on a legal instrument, the 1612/13 mortgage deed for the purchase of the Blackfriars Gatehouse, found among a bundle of title deeds of the family who had bought the property in 1667.[9] At the bottom of the deed are affixed four parchment pendant tags with the signatures of the four executing parties, each tag fastened with a seal.[10] On the first of them is Shakespeare's signature (Fig. 3.2.ii).

The signature is tidier than those on the will, but hardly perfect. Shakespeare, Malone notes, "neglected … to scrape the parchment, in consequence of which the letters appear imperfectly formed." In addition, the signature, Malone observed, was cramped by the narrowness of the tab: "Shakspeare, not finding room for the whole of his name on the label, attempted to write the remaining letters at top, but having allowed himself only room enough to write the letter a, he gave the matter up."[11] Malone had an elegant drawing made of the tag for his 1790 edition, imprinted with a facsimile of the signature, encased within a double border as if to invite its framing (Fig. 3.2.i).

The old crinkly parchment now looks fresh and alive, with the tag slightly flapped over as if by a gentle breeze. A perfected version of the facsimile signature is printed at the bottom of the page, with a caption beneath: "*Shakespeare's Autograph, if it had been written on Paper, would have appeared thus.*" The ink has been blotted, the signature released from spatial constraint. Like a corrupt text, the faulty signature has been restored to its imagined perfection.

All four specimens of Shakespeare's autograph appear on legal instruments found in public or private repositories. Having trained as a barrister, committed "to the study of the law, & the practice of the Court of Chancery," Malone was particularly qualified to search through files and books of record.[12] He spent decades, often alone, collecting documents relating to Shakespeare, in print or in manuscript, usually in transcriptions though he favored originals. Malone scoured through every archive with materials that might bear on Shakespeare, among them: the Chirographer's Office, the Chancery, the Stamp Office, the Tower of London, the Remembrancer's Office, the Exchequer, the College of Arms, the Office of the Lord Chamberlain, the British Museum

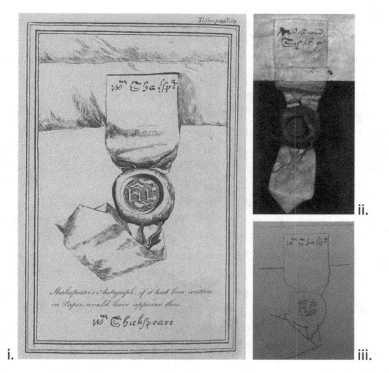

Fig. 3.2 i. Idealized engraving of pendant tag with signature and seal affixed to the Blackfriars Gatehouse mortgage deed, in *The Plays and Poems of William Shakspeare,* ed. Edmond Malone, 10 vols. (1790), I, after 192. **ii.** Pendant tag with signature and seal affixed to the Blackfriars Gatehouse mortgage deed (1613). © Folger Shakespeare Library. **iii.** Copy by William-Henry Ireland of the idealized engraving of the pendant tag (i. above), in Samuel Ireland, *Miscellaneous Papers and Legal Instruments* (1796), preface.

Library and those of Oxford and Cambridge, as well as the libraries and muniments rooms of private homes. He criticized Samuel Johnson, the great biographer of the previous age, for having written *Lives of the Poets* without examining "ancient registers, offices of record and those sepulchers of literature, publick repositories of manuscripts."[13]

His own library served as the repository for the documents he culled, along with the many early quartos he had accumulated of

Shakespeare's plays and those of his contemporaries. His distinction as a Shakespearean was the documentary basis of his work: his first edition of the plays and poems is advertised on the title page as made up of "the most authentick copies," that is, the quartos he believes closest to Shakespeare's manuscript. As we have seen, he conceived of his *Life of Shakspeare* as "compiled of authentick documents," many of which he had previously used to invalidate Rowe's earlier anecdotal accounts. So, too, his *Historical Account of the Rise and Progress of the English Stage* purported "to ascertain the real state of the stage, by the most authentick documents," to the exclusion, as Richard Schoch has demonstrated, of accounts that had been transmitted through theatrical tradition.[14] When possible, he arranged for the actual documents to be delivered to his library, where he held on to them, at times for considerably longer than transcription required. The Stratford parish register, never intended for removal from the parish, was conveyed by coach to his London home (at some risk) on May 15, 1788 and was not returned to the parish until June 25.[15] He borrowed from the office of the Corporation of Stratford three huge folio volumes of their proceedings and held them for twelve years, surrendering them only when the Corporation threatened legal action.[16] Once in his hands, he held on to the Blackfriars Gatehouse deed with Shakespeare's signature (Fig. 3.2.iii) until his death and it did not resurface until 1841.[17] Dulwich Library loaned him what remains the most valuable source of information on the early modern theatre, the theatrical records of the entrepreneur Philip Henslowe, now known as *Henslowe's Diary*. Only after Malone's death were the manuscript pages returned, and in diminished form, for Malone had cut out from its pages a number of signatures of actors and playwrights.[18] He also held on to another item invaluable to the history of the early stage: the Master of the Revels' office-book, a storehouse of information about the licensing and censoring of plays. Because never returned, the office-book is known mainly through copies of Malone's transcriptions.[19] Finally, he allegedly convinced the Keeper of the Ashmolean Library to allow him to remove to his home the unbound sheets of John Aubrey's manuscript of *Brief Lives* and to prohibit others from having access to it.[20] Malone, it might fairly be said, was the self-appointed Keeper of Shakespeare's papers and documents, stowed in his own rooms.

In due course, the documents would be transferred in transcribed form to the capacious volumes of the 1821 variorum edition, completed by James Boswell, Jr. after Malone's death.[21] The plays and poems of that edition are literally encased in documents: at one end are three volumes of "Prolegomena"; at the other, an eighty page Addenda of theatrical documents. In the case of the few documents that had been previously published, Malone claims higher authority for his own copies. Alexander Pope's edition (1723–25) had included a transcription of a draft of the confirmation of Shakespeare's coat of arms from the College of Arms; Malone replaced it with a transcription "copied from the Original in the College of Heralds."[22] The will in Johnson's 1765 edition was, as Malone points out, a transcription of the registered copy, while Malone's was, again, of the original. He considers the list of baptisms Steevens had copied from the Stratford parish register to be "inaccurate and very imperfect," while taking pride in the fidelity of his own, though, as we shall see, he divulges two notable exceptions.

Coleridge, who may himself have been contemplating an edition of Shakespeare, ridiculed Malone as "that eternal Bricker-up of Shakspeare": he had barricaded his works with "Registers, Memorandum Books" of persons whose only distinction was that they were contemporary with Shakespeare: "Bill, Jack, and Harry, Tom, Walter, & Gregory, Charles ... & c & c lived at that time, but ... nothing more is known of them." To Coleridge, the dense exposition—for example, of the wills of six of Shakespeare's fellow players—is pointless pedantry: "half a hundred or more pages though not one word of them by any force can be made to illustrate either the times or life or writings of Shakspeare."[23] Yet for Malone to record the name and date of someone who "lived at that time" was to recover something of Shakespeare. To have been contemporary with Shakespeare—by however many degrees of separation—merited a place in his archive.

**

While Malone's mass of official documents mounted, nothing in Shakespeare's own hand surfaced besides the signatures and they were on impersonal legal instruments. As Malone was quick to point out, the two words, "By me," preceding the last signature on the will did not signify that the will was written by Shakespeare, as the vicar who first located its transcript had believed, finding the style of the dying Shakespeare quite uninspired: "absolutely void of the least particle of that Spirit which Animated Our great Poet."[24] As Malone notes, "'By me,' & c. only means—*The above is the will of me* William Shakspeare."[25]

Of more value would have been letters signed by Shakespeare. Malone, normally skeptical of hearsay, entertains even unlikely rumors of their existence. It was said that some of the "Poet's Letters" had been preserved in the records of the Sackville family, including one in which Shakespeare had written to thank King James for "some bounty" granted him for his Scottish play *Macbeth*. Having heard that the exchange had passed through the hands of the Lord Treasurer, Thomas Sackville, the Earl of Dorset, Malone allows himself "a *bastard* kind of hope that they may really exist." He writes to the Keeper of the Dorset papers inquiring after these "letters of thanks," hoping that "if they indeed exist, they will be dated 1606, or thereabouts" and thereby confirm the date he had assigned *Macbeth* in his chronology.[26]

But it is particularly letters of a more personal cast that Malone was seeking. He is confident that "[a] man of Shakespeare's kindness of heart and friendly disposition" must have written copiously to family and friends during his regular separations from them: "the letters must have been unquestionably voluminous."[27] He comes closest to locating such correspondence after a punishing ten-day examination of the muniments of the Stratford Corporation. On site, and "allowed a complete rummage" of the records, he "unfolded and slightly examined no less than 3000 papers and parchments." The effort yields a happy find: a "very pretty little *relick*, about *three inches long by two broad*," requesting a £30 loan.[28] But it is written to Shakespeare rather than by him: "To my loving good friend and countryman Mr. Wm Shackespere," from his neighbor Richard Quiney, bailiff of Stratford. This letter, still the only correspondence of Shakespeare we have, raises hope of locating what "would have been an *eureka* indeed": Shakespeare's response to Quiney.[29] While the Stratford records yielded specimens of countless hands, Malone's "diligent search" produced not "a single scrap of [Shakespeare's] handwriting." In an unusually affecting sentence, Malone captures his disappointment:

> In looking at this document, which, when folded up, is hardly two inches square, it is impossible not to express an unavailing regret that while this minute memorial of an obscure bailiff of Stratford has come down to us after a lapse of two centuries, uninjured by the accidents of time, we are not in possession of a single manuscript from the pen of his illustrious correspondent.[30]

He feels similarly let down when the medical casebook of Shakespeare's son-in-law, John Hall, is put into his hands. He is certain that Dr. Hall must have tended to Shakespeare during his dying days, but "unluckily the earliest case recorded by Hall is dated in 1617. He had probably filled some other book with memorandums of his practice in preceding years."[31]

Even the key documents he recovers never bring him close enough to Shakespeare.[32] When what is now arguably the most valuable document in early modern theatre history, *Henslowe's Diary*, falls into his hands, his pleasure is qualified: it is for the wrong company and playhouse, for the Lord Admiral's Men at the Rose rather than the King's Men at the Globe, a boon for his history of the stage, but a step removed from Shakespeare. His hope of finding the equivalent for Shakespeare's company is stirred when he locates the will of John Heminges (October 9, 1630), which mentions his "account-books," but they never materialize. Malone recounts how he came upon one of his other major retrievals: Sir Henry Herbert's office-book, which had been mouldering in "an old chest," unopened for 130 years, in the manor house of the Herbert family in Ribbesford, Worcestershire. It also is too far afield. Herbert had been Master of the Revels *after* Shakespeare's death; Malone would have preferred the office-books of Herbert's predecessors, Sir Edmund Tilney and Sir George Buc. At one time, he hoped that he would find that of the latter in the Cottonian Library, since Buc "was a friend of Sir Robert Cotton," but fears it is "irrecoverably lost."[33]

The discovery of Herbert's office-book awakens hope of finding a still more precious book, as he confides to his friend, the literary historian Thomas Warton: "I will not despair of finding Shakespeare's pocketbook."[34] Warton replies sympathetically with the wish that "Shakespeare's Pocket-book will follow." Malone's belief in the existence of such a *vade mecum* may have originated in his autobiographical reading of the Sonnets: "We learn from the 122d sonnet that Shakespeare received a *table-book* from his friend."[35] Sonnet 77 may have led him to expect the pages to be revelatory, like those imagined in the beloved's notebook: "*The vacant leaves thy mind's imprint will bear.*" But if Shakespeare did indeed have a pocketbook or a packet of personal letters, where would they have been put after his death for safekeeping? And to what end? His descendants might well have safeguarded titles to property for purposes of establishing or transferring ownership. But would New Place, Shakespeare's newly purchased home, have kept a repository of manuscript papers, as did the grand ancestral homes of Herbert and Sackville?[36]

***

Earlier in the century, in the preface to his 1733 edition of Shakespeare, Lewis Theobald summarized a recently published notice reporting that "two large Chests full of this Great Man's loose Papers and Manuscripts, in the Hands of an ignorant Baker of *Warwick* (who married one of the Descendants from our Shakespeare), were carelessly scatter'd and thrown about, as Garret-Lumber and Litter, ... till they were all consumed in the general Fire and Destruction of that Town."[37] Theobald is inclined to "distrust the Authority of this Tradition," but not because he doubts the existence of the chests. Rather, he doubts that Shakespeare's wife and daughter would have entrusted the chests to the "ignorant and neglectful Hands" of a remote relative who had married an "ignorant Baker." If they had indeed done so and "if we really lost such a Treasure ... the Misfortune is wholly irreparable." Had the treasure been bequeathed to more responsible hands, his account implies, the chests might have been not "really lost."

Indeed a chest full of Shakespeare's "loose Papers and Manuscripts" does surface, "all in handwriting of Shakespeare," purported to have been found in the unidentified home of an unnamed gentleman.[38] It is not the seasoned scholar and former barrister Malone who brings the cache to light but the junior law clerk William-Henry Ireland. His entire trove was exhibited to visitors at his family home, mainly to great approbation, including by men of considerable antiquarian and literary sophistication. Transcripts and facsimiles of the entire lot were made at great expense and published in *Miscellaneous papers and legal Instruments under the hand and seal of W. Shakespeare* (1796), in both a sumptuous elephantine folio and a modest compact octavo. A table of its contents might have doubled as an inventory of the contents of the fantasized oaken chest: "A letter from Queen Elizabeth" (thanking Shakespeare for writing his Sonnets), "A Note of Hand," a letter and verses to "Anna Hatherreway," "Profession of Faith," "A Letter from Shakspeare to the Earl of Southampton" thanking him for his "greate Bountye" (marked "copye" to explain its presence among the sender's papers), "The Earl of Southampton's Answer," a transcription of the manuscript *The Tragedye of Kynge Leare*, as well as "a Small Fragment of Hamblette."[39] Also included was a Deed of Trust, in which the executor, John Heminges, was instructed to remove the playscripts *"fromm the Oakenn Cheste att our Globe Theatre"* for distribution to Shakespeare's fellow actors: *The Tempest* and *Macbeth* to Richard Cowley, *Cymbeline* and *Coriolanus* to Richard Burbage, *The Comedy of Errors* and *Measure for Measure* to Heminges himself. And there was promise of still more autograph plays to come: "another, and more interesting, historical Play has been discovered amongst the other papers, in the hand writing of Shakspeare," and, rarer still, "a great part of Shakspeare's Library, in which are many books with Notes in his own hand."[40]

Some of these manuscripts might have appeared on Malone's wish list. The preface to *Miscellaneous papers and legal Instruments* concludes with a quotation from Dryden: "nothing [of Shakespeare] should be lost, scarce even 'One drop which fell from Shakspeare's pen.'" In the quotation, the drops of ink are precisely literal, referencing not Shakespeare's dramatic poetry but the actual ink on the page from Shakespeare's quill.[41] The sentence is in fact by Samuel Ireland, William-Henry's father, but it might have been by Malone, who put the same high premium on material in Shakespeare's hand: signatures, personal letters, and play manuscripts.

As the son explains in *The Confessions of William-Henry Ireland* (1805), written after the exposure of his forgeries, he undertook the project to gratify his father. He recalls how he had accompanied him to Stratford on the understanding that "some manuscripts" had been removed for safekeeping from New Place to nearby Clopton House. When they presented themselves there, the current occupant, "a person … devoid of every polished refinement," broke the news that only a fortnight ago, in order to clear a small chamber for some young partridges, he had made a "roaring bonfire" of "several baskets-full of letters and papers," "many bundles with Shakespeare's name wrote upon them." Father and son scoured through the chamber in question and found partridges, but "as to Shakspearian manuscripts, not a line was to be found."[42]

If William-Henry's father gave rise to his son's dream, Malone gave him the means to realize it. According to William-Henry, his father's greatest desire was for Shakespeare's signature. He had heard him "frequently assert, that such was his veneration for the bard that he would willingly give half his library to become possessed even of his signature alone." William-Henry dutifully set about searching for one, rifling through legal papers in the chambers where he clerked and browsing through old vendors' shops and bookstalls. But then another expedient suggested itself: "It was upon perusing an edition of Shakespeare that the idea first struck me of imitating the signature of our bard, in order to gratify Mr. Ireland."[43] That edition was Malone's 1790 *The Plays and Poems of William Shakspeare*, with facsimiles of the four extant signatures, the three on the will taken in 1776 (Fig. 3.1) and the one on the Blackfriars Gatehouse mortgage deed discovered in 1788 (Fig. 3.2.i).[44]

William-Henry got to work, as he later admitted in his *Confessions*, penning a document modeled on the Blackfriars Gatehouse mortgage deed, in a specially concocted dark brown ink on "parchment taken from an old rent-roll," and affixing it with a seal he had cut out from a randomly selected "old deed at chambers" (Fig. 3.3).

According to William-Henry, the first viewer of the "fictious deed" identified the wax impression on the seal as a quintain or "Quintin," a

Fig. 3.3 Drawing by William-Henry Ireland of the "Quintin seal" appendant from the Fraser deed, W. H. Ireland Papers, 1593–1824, MS, Hyde 60 (4). Houghton Library, Harvard University.

device used in tilting practice to test the jouster's control of his spear. That the device formed a visual pun on *Shake-speare* clinched its authenticity: "[F]rom that moment," William-Henry recalled, "the Quintin was gravely affirmed to be the seal always used by our monarch of the drama." The seal's identification had been news to William-Henry who admitted that even had he looked at the stamp on the impress, its significance would have eluded him, it being of "a machine of which I had never heard."[45]

On the basis of the twelve letters he had traced from the facsimile signatures in Malone's edition, William-Henry was able to fashion the rest of the alphabet:

> I formed the twelve different letters contained in the christian and sir names of Wm. Shakspeare as much as possible to resemble the tracings of his original autographs ... The other letters were ideal, and written to correspond as nearly as might be with the general style of the twelve letters used in Shakspeare's names as written by himself.[46]

Yet those twelve letters, as it turned out, were not "as written by [Shakespeare] himself." They were instead as reproduced in Malone's facsimiles. In his hefty monograph exposing Ireland's forgeries, *An Inquiry into the authenticity of certain miscellaneous papers and legal instruments* (1796), Malone explained why the "pretended" signatures resembled the "genuine" ones: "the fabricator had for his direction the autographs with which we have furnished him, and therefore it is not at all surprising that here there should be some little resemblance to the archetypes before him."[47]

A decade later, at the forefront of his *Confessions*, Ireland himself gives evidence of his plagiary by unabashedly reproducing in facsimile two sets of signatures (Fig. 3.4). The first set ("Original Autographs of Shakspeare") is of Ireland's facsimiles of the four facsimile signatures from the will and mortgage deed, as published in Malone's 1790 edition. The second set ("Fictitious Autographs of Shakspeare") is of Ireland's facsimiles of his own forgeries of the 1790 facsimiles, as published in his 1796 *Miscellaneous papers and legal Instruments*.

As it happened, the fabricator's fidelity to Malone's archetypes was his undoing. For as Malone revealed in the course of exposing Ireland's forgeries, two of the letters in Ireland's facsimile signatures replicated mistakes in his own transcriptions.

The first error pertained to the letter *r* on the idealized facsimile of the Blackfriars Gatehouse mortgage autograph with the caption, "*Shakespeare's Autograph, if it had been written on Paper, would have appeared thus*" (Fig. 3.2.i). As Malone now recalls, the engraver, when preparing to incise that signature on the steel plate, asked Malone "to furnish him with an 'archetype' for the letter r." Lacking any specimens in type, Malone "inadvertently took down a MS. of [Shakespeare's] time, which happened to be near at hand, and pointed out to him a German r":

[𝖗.] Yet as Malone here maintains, Shakespeare uniformly signed his name in a secretary hand. The presence of the alien *r* in Ireland's papers proved "implicitly" that they were not written by Shakespeare but copied from Malone's doctored facsimile of the mortgage deed. Even if intended, Malone adds, he could not have set a better "trap for this fabricator to fall into."[48]

With the same mortgage deed signature, Malone inadvertently set a second trap. When in 1776 he had examined with Steevens the three signatures on the will, he thought the third of them (Fig. 3.1) read "Shakspeare." When he discovered the cramped signature on the mortgage deed tab (Fig. 3.2.ii), he imagined it consisted of the same letters and his engraver clearly reproduced it as such: *ꞟ Ꝑ Shakspeare* . But now, decades later, in both his *Inquiry* as well as in his *Life*, Malone discloses that he had misread both signatures: the turn or curl he "formerly

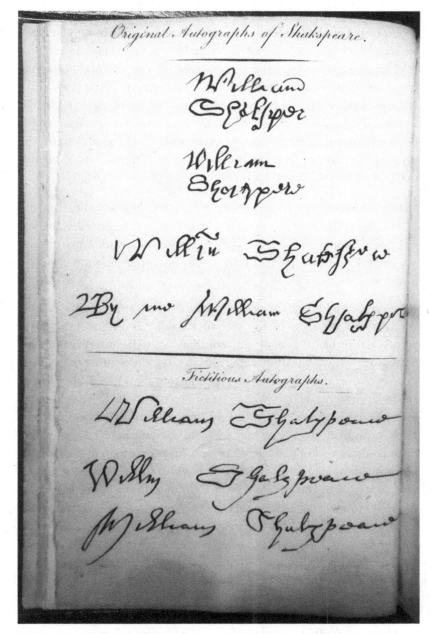

Fig. 3.4 Facsimiles by William-Henry Ireland of the "Original" and "Fictitious" autographs of Shakespeare, *The Confessions of William-Henry Ireland* (1805) after preface.

supposed to be that letter *a* over [the mortgage] autograph ... was only a coarse broad mark of a contraction" of the letters *e* and *r*. In sum, Malone, by his own admission, had mistranscribed two of the seven miniscules of Shakespeare's surname on the mortgage deed. To the end of exposing the forger or "fabricator" as he terms him, Malone steps deeper into error. He argues that Shakespeare consistently spelled his surname with an *a* in the second syllable, thereby contradicting his own disquisition on the orthographic inconsistency of proper names in Shakespeare's time. Any Shakespeare autograph at variance with the spelling *Shakspere*, he now generalizes, is a de facto forgery:[49]

[I]t is manifest that he wrote it himself SHAKSPERE; and therefore if any original Letter or other MS. of his shall ever be discovered, his name will appear in that form. The necessary consequence is, that these papers, in which a different orthography is almost uniformly found, cannot but be a forgery.[50]

Yet astonishingly Malone peremptorily resolves to continue writing the name (with an *a* in the second syllable) as he insisted Shakespeare never had: "I shall still continue to write our poet's name SHAKSPEARE."[51] Malone defends his decision by arguing that *Shakspeare* was the original and correct spelling, but the *a* had dropped from *speare* to conform with the abbreviated "Shaksper" and "Shaksp" as well as the elided *Shakspere*. The *a*-less spelling of *speare,* he speciously maintains, is an instance not so much of "old spelling as of false spelling," and should be prohibited in the present: "in my opinion it ought not to be adopted in exhibiting our author's name at this day; and therefore I write *Shakspeare,* and not *Shakspere.*" Thus the editor whose edition purported to follow Shakespeare's texts "*verbatim*" goes his own way in the very spelling of his author's surname. He gives a specious philological explanation for holding fast to a spelling he believes Shakespeare never used, but which he himself had followed in everything on Shakespeare he had published to date, including his ten-volume edition of *The Plays and Poems of William Shakspeare* (1790).

As Malone points out, his invalidation of Ireland's signatures alone "without any other consideration, would prove beyond a doubt the forgery of the whole heterogeneous mass."[52] If the "archetype" of the signature is corrupt, so too will be the papers and instruments modeled on it. Every "German r" in Ireland's forgeries would point to the handwriting's origin in Malone's faulty transcription; any signature divergent from "Shakspere" was a fabrication. All the same, Malone devotes 400 pages to sedulously inspecting and invalidating each of the nineteen items in the fabricator's "whole heterogeneous mass." Clearly, it is of paramount importance to sharply differentiate his authentic materials from Ireland's "pretended" papers and instruments that were generated from them. Yet scholar and forger share the same fixation on writing in Shakespeare's hand. The latter fabricates the autograph papers the former had sought in vain to discover.

At the close of Malone's exposure of Ireland's forgeries in *An Inquiry* comes a call for original papers. A three-page prospectus announces Malone's forthcoming "New life based on authentick documents" and requests that any relevant materials be brought forward. It is hoped that materials will be drawn "from some hitherto unexplored Repository papers ... of a very different complexion from the miserable trash we have now been examining." And yet this quest, like the Irelands' journey to Stratford, presumes that Shakespeare's papers had been stowed away, whether in the fictitious "oaken chest" or in the "unexplored Repository," unopened since the time of their imagined stowage. In the prospectus, the records are imagined to have descended through Shakespeare's family line until reaching Shakespeare's last direct descendant, his granddaughter, Lady Barnard, whose kinsman and executor was a Mr. Edward Bagley: "This person ... must have become possessed of all her Coffers and Cabinets, in which undoubtedly were several of her [great] Grandfather's Papers." Or perhaps the coffers and cabinets remained in New Place with her husband and then after his death with her stepdaughters, who were entitled by her will to remain in the house for another six months: "some of the Poet's Papers might have fallen into their hands."[53]

Both Malone's 1821 variorum edition and Ireland's 1796 boxed folio of *Miscellaneous Papers and Instruments* are bibliographic surrogates for that imaginary chest: repositories of the desired play manuscripts, letters, and notes in Shakespeare's own hand. Malone's twenty-one volume edition laden with "authentick documents," discovered and collected by him, and Ireland's Folio stashed with fabricated documents of his own making are driven by the same desire for proximity to Shakespeare. Both scholar and forger are driven by what Roger Chartier calls "the fetishism of the author's hand," the late-eighteenth-century desire for materials in the author's own hand, exacerbated in the case of Shakespeare by their near absence.[54]

***

In Theobald's account, it is an "ignorant Baker" who is responsible for destroying the cache of Shakespeare's papers; in Ireland's, "a person ... devoid of every polished refinement." For Malone, it is the generations between himself and Shakespeare: "The truth is, our ancestors paid very little attention to posterity: they thought many things trifles, and not worthy of notice ... and have left us in the dark."[55] Even record-keepers during this interval, according to Malone, treated records as ephemera. Unable to find a record of Shakespeare's marriage, he suspects that the books of registry once replete with entries were tossed and replaced: "The ancient registers of Weston and Billesley having, like most other ancient registers, been thrown by and lost, as soon as they were filled with names, and it became necessary to procure a new blank book" (II, 117). Then there's Shakespeare's elusive birthdate; the month and year were established, but the day had to be taken, as we have seen, "on faith of Mr. Green, but *quaere*, how did Mr. Green ascertain this fact? (II, 63). The omitting to mention the day of the child's birth in baptismal registers, is a great defect, as the knowledge of this fact is often of importance" (II, 63, n6). That anything remains at all of Shakespeare's life is the result not of any solicitude on the part of those who lived after him, but of sheer accident, and, of course, Malone's own unstinting "biographical researches": "we must content ourselves with such particulars as accident has preserved, or the most sedulous industry has been able to collect" (II, 4).

And so it is that his *Life of Shakspeare* begins with a bleak reckoning of all those "who lived nearer to our author's time" and might have left records behind but did not. He unabashedly singles them out by name for their "negligence and inattention" (II, 11). His biography opens with a long indictment: "A large list of persons presents itself, from whom, without doubt, much intelligence concerning [Shakespeare] might have been obtained" (II, 7). Here are a few highlights from his eight pages of un-acknowledgment.

SHAKESPEARE'S ARCHIVE   81

There is William Dugdale, the antiquary who lived only twenty miles from Stratford and whose life overlapped with Shakespeare's for over a decade. From him, "we might reasonably have expected some curious memorial of his illustrious countryman: but he has not given us a single particular of his life"—only a "very slight mention" (II, 4).

Then there is another antiquary, Anthony Wood, who lived only thirty-six miles from Stratford and was born only fourteen years after Shakespeare's death. Why hadn't Wood included an account in his *Athenæ Oxonienses. An exact history of all the writers and bishops who have had their education in the most ancient and famous University of Oxford, from ... 1500 to the end of ... 1690* (1691-2). Never mind that Shakespeare never had matriculated: Wood, Malone maintains, "could have easily found a niche for [Shakespeare's] Life"—or slipped it into the niche of the Life of an alumnus, Sir William Davenant, for example (II, 5).

Malone also calls John Dryden to task for not having collected any personal details: "Dryden might have obtained some intelligence from the old actors who died about the time of the Restoration, when he was himself near thirty years old" (II, 7). Had either Dryden, Davenant, or the actor Thomas Betterton taken the trouble to visit the poet's youngest daughter, who lived till 1662, or his granddaughter, who did not die till 1670, many particulars might have been preserved which are now irrecoverably lost; "some *letters* at least she surely must have had" (II, 623). Indeed, none of Shakespeare's relations seem to have thought of posterity: not his sister Joan Hart, alive until 1646; nor his eldest daughter, Susanna Hall, alive until 1649, nor his second daughter, Judith Queeny, alive until 1662.

Finally, Malone supplied a numbered list "of those who were not thus nearly connected with our poet ... but from whom, without doubt, much intelligence concerning him might have been obtained" (II, 7). Number six on his list of the negligent are three generations of Verneys: Richard Verney, who died at ninety in 1711, might have "made some inquiries" of his father, who lived from 1588 to 1642, as his father should have made of his father, who lived from 1563 to 1630 and who served as Justice of the Peace in Stratford around the elusive time of Shakespeare's departure for London.

That almost a century had elapsed without any attempt to recover anything about Shakespeare's private life or literary career; that when the attempt was made it was so poorly executed (by Rowe)—and then reproduced to the satisfaction of the public for eighty years—until Malone took it upon himself to write a life compiled of authentic documents: these were all "circumstances which cannot be contemplated without astonishment ... The negligence and inattention of our English writers after the Restoration ... can never be mentioned without surprise and indignation" (II, 11–12).

It falls upon Malone to make up for his predecessors' neglect through his biographical researches at a distance of almost two centuries. But however much his "diligent and ardent spirit of inquiry" might recover, he cannot make up for the laxity of his predecessors: "it must, however, necessarily be accompanied with a deep, though unavailing regret, that the same ardour did not animate those who lived nearer our author's time, whose inquiries could not fail to have been rewarded with a superior degree of success" (II, 11). So pervasive was the indifference that he ascribes it to the era itself. Like the so-called Dark Ages separating the Renaissance from antiquity, the period between himself and Shakespeare "was not an age of curiosity or inquiry" (II, 7):

> The truth is, our ancestors paid very little attention to posterity: they thought many things trifles, and unworthy of notice, which we consider important ... . The biographer of our poet has, above all others, especial reason to lament the literary penury of his contemporaries, whose admiration of his genius, high as it was, never led them to transmit to posterity any particulars of his private life, or dramatick history. (II, 211, n.2).

In his indictment of the lax generations before him, Malone spares two seventeenth-century writers: Gerard Langbaine and John Aubrey. He applies himself to the work of both men, scrupulously annotating Langbaine's octavo survey of plays, *An Account of the English Dramatick Poets* (1691), and painstakingly transcribing John Aubrey's baggy manuscript compilation now known as *Brief Lives* (c. 1669–96). The basis of Malone's attraction is obvious: both writers produce works consisting of records assembled from disparate sources and brimming with names and dates. The Bodleian Library, where Malone's Shakespearean materials were reposited, holds the result of his engagement with both works: his copy of Langbaine's octavo, unstitched, interleaved, and bound in four volumes, with annotations (his own and those copied from three previous scholars), and two folio notebooks comprising his transcription, annotations, and sorting of 174 of Aubrey's manuscript lives.[56]

Yet there are limits to Malone's appreciation. He is troubled by both Langbaine's system and Aubrey's ostensible lack of one. Langbaine had "adopted a very absurd method; that of arranging [the plays] alphabetically."[57] Aubrey, he complains, did not "methodize his papers" at all.[58] Malone's commitment to chronology blinds him to both the alphabetical organization of the one and the adventitious layout of the other.

Gerard Langbaine's 550-page *An Account of the English Dramatick Poets* (1691) is a compendium of almost a thousand plays in English by over two hundred playwrights up to the time of its writing, with accompanying biographic, bibliographic, and critical commentary. As Langbaine's capacious subtitle indicates, genre is key: *Some Observations and Remarks on the Lives and Writings of all those that have Publish'd either Comedies, Tragedies, Tragi-Comedies, Pastorals, Masques, Interludes, Farces, or Opera's in the English Tongue.*[59] After each play title, its generic assignment typically follows. But the compendium is arranged not generically, like the seventeenth-century folios, or chronologically, like the 1821 Malone–Boswell edition, but alphabetically. Two alphabetized indices enframe the compendium: an index of "The Authors Names" at the front and an "Alphabetical Index of Plays" at the back. "William Shakespear" is alphabetized like any other author, though Langbaine claims to "esteem his Plays beyond any that have ever been published in our Language" (454). His sixteen-page entry appears between "Thomas Shadwell" and "Lewis Sharpe" and includes the forty-three plays of the Third and Fourth Folios. Once alphabetized, the seven plays appended to the 1663/4 and 1685 folios can be seamlessly incorporated into the original Folio corpus. Comments follow most titles—on the play's publication and performance as well as "other Observations, which might *obiter* occur or relate more immediately to each Play" (Preface).

To readers accustomed to seeing the plays in the generic order of the seventeenth-century folios or the chronological one of modern editions of the collected works, the alphabetical arrangement looks quite odd: *Coriolanus* follows *The Comedy of Errors*, *Titus Andronicus* comes after *The Tempest*, and *Othello* after *Oldcastle*. But Langbaine's compendium, like any lexically organized work, is not intended to be read sequentially, one entry after another. Nor are the entries to be read in isolation, for the commentary repeatedly directs the reader from one entry to another, and the two alphabetical indices enable the navigation. The entry for *Coriolanus*, for example, notes that a version of the play had recently been staged "under the Title of Ingratitude of a Common-Wealth" (455). After consulting that title under the "Alphabetical Index of Plays" and discovering the play's author to be "Nathaniel [*sic*] Tate," the reader can then flip ahead to his entry to learn that "generally [Tate] follows other Mens Models, and builds upon their Foundations: for of Eight Plays that are printed under his Name, Six of them owe their Original to other Pens" (500). The entries identify those six plays and their "Models": three are modeled on plays by "Shakespear" and the other three on plays by "Fletcher," "Jonson," and "Sir Aston Cokain." The reader might well be familiar with the dramatists who comprise the English dramatic triumvirate, but who, she might ask, was "Sir Aston"? Flipping back into the volume, she would find a four-page entry on his lineage, education, and travels as well as titles for three plays, a masque, and various other poetical pieces. In addition, she would learn that he too built on "other Mens Models," so that *The Obstinate Lady*, for example, "seems to be Cousin-German to Massinger's *Very Woman*" (69). If still keen, she might then follow the lead to "Massinger" and learn that while Langbaine cannot identify the play on which *Very Woman* was founded (358), he can give wide-ranging sources for other plays by Massinger, among them the histories of Suetonius, the poems of Valerius Maximus, the "Italian Novels" of Boccaccio, and the chronicles of Speed and Stow. Thus, the reader who dips into the volume to find out about *Coriolanus* is prompted to crisscross from one entry to another, guided through the expanse of English dramatic writing by Langbaine's indexical system.

Like Massinger, Shakespeare also founded plays on the Roman historians, the English chroniclers, and the Italian and French novelists. When Langbaine cannot provide the "Original" for one of Shakespeare's plays, it is not because there is none, but because he hasn't yet come upon it. "I know not whence our Author fetch'd his Story," he admits of *Pericles* (462); of *Hamlet*, he gives the reader a few hints of where to look. As Shakespeare drew on other writers, so after the Interregnum others drew on him. As the reader learns when perusing the "Shakespear" entry, *Cymbeline* was "reviv'd" by Thomas Durfey, *Henry VI Part 2* by John Crown, *King Lear* and *Coriolanus* by Tate, *Titus* by Edward Ravenscroft, *Measure for Measure* and *Much Ado* by Davenant, *Timon* by Thomas Shadwell, and *The Tempest* and *Troilus* by Dryden.

Not only did modern English dramatic poets (on either side of the Interregnum) "make use" of earlier models: so, too, did the ancients, and Langbaine insists in defending Ben Jonson's appropriation of them. Jonson, "in borrowing from the Ancients, has only follow'd the pattern the Romans themselves had set" (145). As Jonson built on the Romans, so the Romans did on the Greeks:

> Thus *Seneca* in his Tragedies imitated *Euripides*, and *Aeschylus*; *Terence* borrow'd from *Menander*, and in his Prologue to *Andria*, quotes *Naevius, Plautus, and Ennius* for his Authority. I could enumerate more Instances, but these are sufficient Precedents to excuse Mr. *Johnson*. (147)

So Langbaine canvasses a long and wide dramatic field, finding precedent and defence for modern practices of playwriting.

As our present chronological schema encourages a reading of the plays in terms of Shakespeare's development and the Folio's generic classification invited comparisons of Shakespeare with the ancients, so Langbaine's indexical system linked Shakespeare to a sprawling nexus of writers before and after him, those he drew on and those who drew on him. Langbaine's survey is comprehensive, but not in the sense that it covers plays in England from the beginning of the English dramatic tradition to the time of its writing. *An Account* has no starting point. The earliest English playwrights in his compendia are "[t]wo Authors that liv'd in the Reign of Queen Elizabeth," Thomas Sackville and Thomas Norton, and they are introduced at the very close of the work and in a short appendix, "thro' oversight omitted in the Body of the *Book*".

Nor is there a definitive endpoint. Indeed, while Langbaine goes "as far as this present Time," his survey concludes with an open invitation to future readers: "Thus I have finish'd My ACCOUNT ... and having laid a Foundation, I shall leave it to Others ... to perfect the Edifice" (Appendix).[60] Malone takes up this invitation in his own *Historical Account of the Rise and Progress of the English Stage*, with the aim not of extending Langbaine's schema but of laying down a very different one, organized by advancing dates rather than indexical letters. To this end, Langbaine turned out to be of little help. Malone repeatedly targets Langbaine's dates, supplying missing ones (for the quartos of *Pericles*, *Richard II*, and *Richard III*, for example) and correcting erroneous ones, including that of Shakespeare's birth.[61] Two antiquaries whose notes on Langbaine are transcribed by Malone into his own copy also regret the inaccuracy of his dates. "A woeful Chronologist art thou, Gerard Langbaine!" complained the antiquarian William Oldys. Because Langbaine's dates are for the editions he owns or has seen, rather than for first editions, they have been a "perpetual source of confusion ... and occasion constant anachronisms," according to another antiquarian colleague, Thomas Percy. Had Langbaine known the dates when a play was first published or performed, he suspects, he might well have listed the authors and their works accordingly: "It was probably owing to the difficulty he found in discovering the first editions that our author chose to distribute the works of each person alphabetically, rather than dispose them (more naturally) in the order of time in which they were severally written."[62] But, as we have seen, Langbaine's interest lies not in tracking the gradual rise of English dramatic writing but in demonstrating the reticulations across time of English dramatic works that are either modeled on the works of others or serve themselves as models, or both.

Langbaine's alphabetical method, however absurd to Malone, is designed to enable the reader to weave in and out of the volume's 254 entries, ricocheting from one entry to another, looping both backwards and forwards in the volume, following linkages across time, language, and genre that make up, for him, the warp and weft of English dramatic writing. His is a history of drama without growth, maturity, development; if anything, there is a falling off on Langbaine's side of the Interregnum. These plays hew too closely to their models, written in the same language, replicating the same genre, often duplicating the same words. "Modern *Plagiaries*," he terms them (Preface). Shakespeare and his cohort, by contrast, go further afield both linguistically and generically, borrowing from Greek, Roman, French, and Italian histories, plays, and romances. As a chronological schema encourages a reading of the plays in terms of Shakespeare's development, Langbaine's alphabetization weaves the plays into an expansive dramatic tradition. Shakespeare is one thread in the complex fabric, tied to other playwrights by his imitation of them and by theirs of him.

Malone invests even more time and effort in his transcription and annotation of John Aubrey's *Brief Lives* or *Minutes of Lives* and here, too, the returns are limited. On July 10, 1792, he records in his notebook his intention to prepare an edition of Aubrey and on September 16, 1792, he records his having begun the project.[63] According to one report, he intended this edition to be "on the same scale as his last edition of Shakespear," published in 1790.[64] As Kate Bennett, Aubrey's latest editor, observes, Aubrey's *Brief Lives* is "an inchoate manuscript, never intended for print."[65] There is little physical uniformity to its content: pages vary in size from folio to snippet, some stitched together, others interleaved, and some pinned to larger pages. The pages are mainly in manuscript (though some have been excised from printed texts) and in Aubrey's hand (though some are in those of his correspondents). Different genres of inscription intermix: printed pamphlets, poems, epitaphs, bibliographies, letters, seals, and horoscopes. There are also sketches (some colored in) of armorial crests, tombs, gardens, buildings, inventions. Every page includes marginal notes running smack into the text proper, as well as insertions, deletions, interlinear writing, blank spaces, sometimes for a missing name or date, sometimes for an entire life. Aubrey deposited the unbound pages in the Ashmolean in 1693, where they were stored in a two-foot-square basement cabinet, untouched until the end of the eighteenth century.

The extreme heterogeneity of Aubrey's compilation seems to militate against its conversion into a printed book. Bennett describes the manuscripts as "paper museums" for the variety and rarity of their material content.[66] Before Malone's transcriptions, only nine of the lives had appeared in print, in a lavishly printed volume entitled *The Oxford Cabinet*, after its basement provenance.[67] Aubrey maintained that because he had not made a fair copy of *Lives*, the manuscripts would survive "in puris naturalibus," in their true colors, unmediated by print, and this, he adds, "pleases an antiquary."[68] Put to paper by several hands, over a period of some forty years, generically miscellaneous and never finished, the manuscript posed a daunting editorial challenge: how to marshal so much messy stuff into a printed book. Not until 1860 were the manuscripts paginated, stitched and bound into three volumes, though not in the order in which Aubrey had delivered them to the Ashmolean.[69] Earlier editors had intervened, foremost among them being Malone, who according to Bennett had "a very active role in shaping the *Lives* manuscripts into their current form." One of the three bound volumes is "substantially Malone's creation" made up of materials by Aubrey from other manuscripts which Malone believed belonged in *Brief Lives*.[70] He also inserted a parchment title page identifying their content: "These scattered fragments collected and arranged by E M. Sep. 1792."[71] We cannot know whether during the long period in which he kept the manuscript he in any way rearranged the pages of the other two volumes. We can, however, know how he would have arranged them had he realized his intention to publish an edition.

As is apparent from his two volumes of transcriptions in the Bodleian, Malone's first editorial fiat was to divide the assorted manuscript sheets into two categories: Part I, *Containing the Lives of the Poets*, and Part II, *Containing the Lives of Prose Writers and other celebrated persons*. For each of the two sections, he devises a table of contents in which he lists the lives in chronological order (from the date of death). Here, too, the influence of Priestley's *A Chart of Biography* makes itself felt. Indeed Priestley's dated timelines or biographs might have been Malone's source for some of the dates he supplies or corrects in Aubrey. The poets range from Chaucer to Edmund Waller (Fig. 3.5).

The prose writers extend from the thirteenth-century Roger Bacon to John Wilkins and Isaac Barrow (Fig. 3.6), both contemporaries of Aubrey and, like Aubrey, fellows of the Royal Society. Malone follows this chronological lineup when he transcribes the lives on the recto pages of the two notebooks, with his own annotations on the verso,

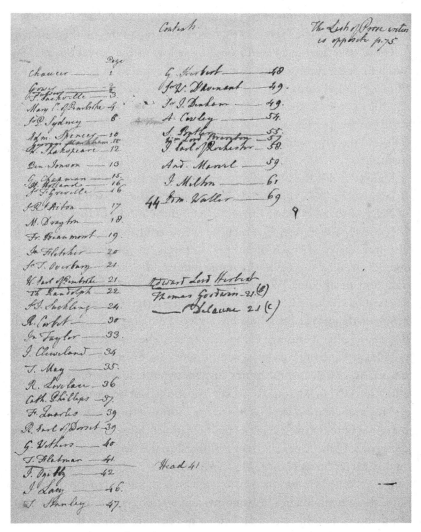

Fig. 3.5 Chronological list of the "Lives of the Poets," prepared by Edmond Malone for his transcription of John Aubrey's *Brief Lives*, MS, Eng. Misc. d. 26, 1v. © Bodleian Libraries, University of Oxford.

keyed to the transcription by ciphers. One of the casualties of Malone's chronological rearrangement is its repositioning of the mathematician, scientist, and astrologer and founding fellow of the Royal Society, Sir William Petty. Aubrey had "from the first" intended to give Petty pride of place and accords him the most elaborately decorated page, with a carefully copied and colored image of his heraldic escutcheon as well as a full horoscope (Fig. 3.7).[72] That preeminence is lost, however, when he falls into the unremarkable fifty-second place of Malone's chronological lineup.

Malone is not the only editor who attempted to methodize Aubrey's *Brief Lives*. In 1898 Andrew Clark, the editor of the first scholarly edition of *Brief Lives*, resorted to the alphabet, on the model of the *Dictionary of National Biography*, to which he was a contributor (as A.C-k). He also introduced for each of Aubrey's subjects, the biographical formula standardized by the *DNB*: the name followed by the parenthetic birthdate and deathdate: "William Shakespear (1564–1616)."[73] Only Kate Bennett has followed "the order of the manuscript, folio by folio." While acknowledging that the whole has suffered damage and alteration both before and after its storage in the Ashmolean, she discerns traces of a few possible organizing rubrics, a run of poets, for example, and of mathematicians, as well as some minor clusters around family circles or college affiliations.[74] For Malone, however, chronological order overrides even Aubrey's single most explicit instruction for ordering the lives, Aubrey's marginal notes to the life of the mathematician John Pell: "I would have the Lives of John Dee, Sir Henry Billingsley, the two Digges, father and sonne, Mr Thomas Hariot, Mr .... Warner, Mr Brigges, and Dr. Pell, be putt together."[75] Common to all seven men is an interest in the congruent subjects of mathematics, astronomy, and astrology. Malone ignores the stipulation: "But this direction I could not comply with, as it would have interfered with the chronological arrangement ... I have endeavored to *preserve*" (italics added).[76] Perhaps he intended *observe* rather than *preserve* here, for there is no chronological arrangement in Aubrey's *Brief Lives* to preserve.

In Aubrey, as in Langbaine, Malone is attracted to dates. Many of his annotations correct Aubrey's dates or supply those he omitted. In his

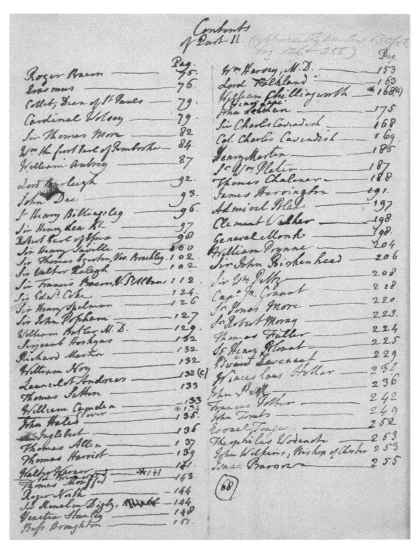

Fig. 3.6 Chronological list of the "Lives of Prose Writers and Other Celebrated Persons," prepared by Edmond Malone for his transcription of John Aubrey's *Brief Lives*, MS, Eng. Misc. d. 26, 75v. © Bodleian Libraries, University of Oxford.

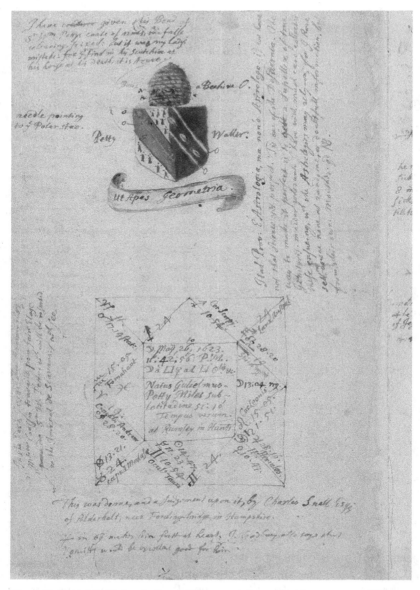

Fig. 3.7 Sketch by John Aubrey of the escutcheon and horoscope of Sir William Petty, *Brief Lives*, MS, Aubrey 6, f. 12v. © Bodleian Libraries, University of Oxford.

transcriptions, he supplies those for Francis Beaumont, Mary Countess of Pembroke, Sir Thomas Overbury, John Sackville, Catherine Philips, and numerous others. In a few cases, where Aubrey had left a blank or dotted line, Malone actually inserts the date into the manuscript proper. In John Suckling's entry, Aubrey writes, "He was born...," and Malone fills in the ellipsis with "1612," before crossing it out and inserting "in the year 1609": "This date I have supplied. It appears from the Register of the Parish of Twickeham." Aubrey had calculated that Suckling was 28 when he died: "This however was a mistake," and Malone emends it from the same registry. In the entry for the mathematician William Oughtred, he again corrects Aubrey, who records his age as "eighty eight + odde dayes": "This is a mistake in computation. Having been born on March 5, 1574–5, he was in March 1660 but eighty-five complete and consequently died in his 86th yr." Aubrey leaves blank the final digit of the poet John Cleveland—"He died of the ... AD 165_"—while Malone both supplies the missing digit "8" and alters the cause of death: "This is a mistake. He died of an intermitting fever."[77] Malone is particularly proud of having ascertained the date Aubrey could not live to provide: that of Aubrey's own death, previously only estimated at "about the year 1700": "I this day, however, found that he was buried in St. Mary Magdalen's church or churchyard Oxon June 7 1697."[78] (As was his practice, he also registers the date of his discovery: "July 18, 1792.")

Aubrey above all is interested in the birthdate, though not as the starting point of a continuous biographical narrative. The birthdate is essential for the casting of a geniture or astrological nativity. In writing to a colleague, he stressed its importance: "I would have all their Nativities religiously sett downe (if attainable) as also their Obijt's, for the sake and improvement of Astrologie."[79] As he makes clear in his prefatory letter to his antiquarian colleague Anthony Wood, his interest in biography was impelled by the conviction that it would be "of great use for the advancement of Astrology":

[W]e have not that Science yet perfect. 'Tis one of the Desiderata. The way to make it perfect is to get a Supellex of true Genitures. in order whereunto I have with much care collected these ensueing, which the Astrologers may rely-on.[80]

"Supellex" is a Baconian term for a stockpile of raw "stuff," signaling Aubrey's adherence to the Baconian ideal by which knowledge begins with the accumulation of empirical data—the more the better.[81] In this instance, that data is assembled by collecting individual horoscopes. Ideally, it would include the place and time of birth *up to the minute*, the smallest division of time before the seconds measured by the mechanical clocks of the next century. Aubrey's occasional reference to his collection as *Minutes of Lives* captures the brevity or minuteness of its entries, but it also invokes the smallest temporal measure by which the astral conjunctions presiding over a nativity and influencing a life are determined.[82]

In Malone's transcript, no traces of Aubrey's twenty-odd envelope horoscopes remain, though he does avail himself of their birthdates. In the entry for the philosopher Desiderius Erasmus, for example, he has lifted the birthdate out of the center of Aubrey's natal diagram and inserted it into his text: "He was born at Rotterdam Oct. 27, 1467." So, too, he draws the poet Edmund Waller's birthdate up from the astrological chart at the bottom of Aubrey's page to the top of his own transcription: "he was born ... on the 3d day of March 1605-6." On several occasions, Malone faults Aubrey for not distancing himself from the astrological excesses of his subjects. In his Life of John Dee, Aubrey relates reports of Dee's conjuring: "he shewed the Eclipse with a darke Roome ... kept a great many Stilles goeing ... he layd the Storme."[83] This, Malone notes, was evidence of Aubrey's superstitious "weak side," and he marvels "that [Aubrey] should mention the vagaries of [Dee's] *supernatural* assertions without reprobation."[84] His own reprobation surfaces in his note on Aubrey's description of Cleveland as "a comely plump man, good curled hair, dark brown": "Soft or Flaccid hair was thought an unfavourable denotation by those idle enough to put any confidence in astrology." Stronger antipathy still follows upon Aubrey's description of John Pell's "melancholio-sanguine dark brown hair, with an excellent moist curl":[85] "Here our author is *at his old lunes.*"[86]

Malone sidelines Aubrey's astrological interest as if it were an incidental quirk irrelevant to his lives and therefore quite expendable. But a horoscope is, for Aubrey, a kind of encrypted blueprint of a life—and nowhere more than in the life Aubrey writes of himself, centred around his completed horoscopic envelope as if emanating out from there (Fig. 3.8).

He describes his own life as "remarqueable in an Astrologicall respect," for from his birth to his later years, he has suffered under the influence of unhappily conjoined planets: "Labouring under a Crowd of ill Directions."[87] Life begins in ill health: "Borne 12 March about Sun-riseing ... being very weake and like to dye" and so baptized straight away. Up until the age of twelve, he experiences "sicknesse of vomiting, Belly ake, paine in the side." Within half a year of grammar school, his favorite tutor has died and he is put in the hands of dull, ignorant, and ill-natured teachers. His education at Oxford is interrupted by war and ill health so that he is forced into the countryside: "It was a most sad life to me, then in the prime of my youth, not to have the benefit of an ingeniose Conversation and scarce any good books." His father's death leaves him with crushing debts and lawsuits. He loses the woman he intends to marry, as well as her considerable fortune. To his "inexpressible griefe and ruine," his mother prevents him from seeing the antiquities of Italy. "I was in as much affliction as a mortall could be." Impecunious and peripatetic, "from 1649 to 1670, never off my horseback," he wishes the old religious houses still survived, "that Monasterys had not been putt downe": "what a pleasure 'twould have been to have travelled from Monastery to Monastery .... Strange Fate, that I have labourd under: never in my life to enjoy one entire Moneths otium or Contemplation." And yet, still "notwistanding all these embarassments, I did pian piano (as they occurd) tooke notes of Antiq[uities]."[88] Those notes became the contents of his numerous studies, including his *Brief Lives*: fifty years hence, he predicted, those lives would themselves be considered antiquities.[89]

In a letter prefacing *Brief Lives*, Aubrey describes the happenstance nature of his work, explaining that he has "putt in writing these Minutes of LIVES, tumultuarily, as they occurr'd to my thoughts or as occasionally I had information of them."[90] In this respect, the *Minutes* follow the fortuitous course of his own bumpy and ill-starred life: "of this over halfe a Centurie of years ... much tumbled up and downe in it."

In transcribing the life of the poet Edmund Waller, Malone records that he has transferred a paragraph in Aubrey's manuscript from the end of the entry to its middle and then justifies the move: "Mr. Aubrey put

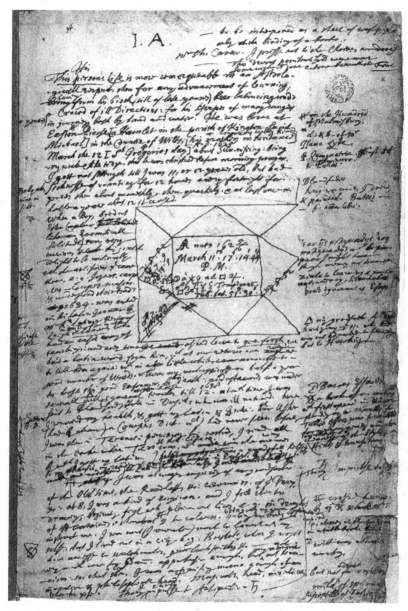

Fig. 3.8 Draft by John Aubrey of his own Life and horoscope, *Brief Lives*, MS Aubrey 7, f. 3. © Bodleian Libraries, University of Oxford.

down his information as he could obtain it, and did not live to methodize his papers."[91] If only Aubrey had lived longer than his long life of seventy-two years, Malone must be thinking, he might have found the time to sort his *Brief Lives* systematically. But more likely Aubrey wanted his *Lives* to remain largely in that tumultuous layout, true to how he happened upon his materials as well as to how things befell in the lives he put to paper.

Langbaine's published survey, *An Account of the English Dramatick Poets*, and Aubrey's manuscript assemblage, *Brief Lives*, might at first blush be taken for the kind of repositories Malone was seeking for his projected biographical narrative composed of authentic documents. In their amassing and processing of materials from disparate sources, Langbaine and Aubrey seem to share his modern record-keeping impulse rather than the laxity Malone attributed to their earlier age. Yet both compilations fall short of expectation: Langbaine's alphabetical criss-crossing strikes Malone as absurd; Aubrey's adventitious disposition calls for rational chronologizing. As the attempt to narrate a Life (1564–1611) largely dispensed with the undated anecdotes in Chapter 1, as the dedication to Shakespeare's chronology preempted ancient genre in Chapter 2, so, too, the exclusive focus on authorial documents ruled out earlier more diffusive forms of record.

The search for Shakespeare's archive began as a fantasy of a long-lost strongbox of some kind—a chest, cabinet, or coffer—in which the desired personal papers were supposed to have been prudently stowed. The legacy, it was imagined, had at Shakespeare's death been left intact but was subsequently squandered or lost by those who should have secured its transmission. With the exception of Ireland's forgeries, however, nothing of what it was imagined to contain ever turned up: no personal letters, no diary, no notes, no manuscripts of his works, in draft or in final state. It was in the context of this impossible longing for Shakespeare's absent firsthand materials that the 1609 *Sonnets* were first canonized. They were not written in Shakespeare's own hand, of course. They were, however, composed in his own voice—at least, that was the assumption on which the first critical edition of the Sonnets (1780) was predicated.

4

The "deceasèd I" of the 1609 *Sonnets*

Upon opening the 1609 quarto of *Shake-speares Sonnets*, an early reader might be forgiven for thinking Shakespeare was dead. The only front matter between its title page and the first sonnet is a dedication page printed to resemble an epitaph. The typography is modeled on ancient lapidary tablets incised in Roman square capitals known as *capitalis monumentalis*, the easiest to carve in stone. As with the ancient inscriptions, words are separated not with spaces but with interpuncts (Fig. 4.1).

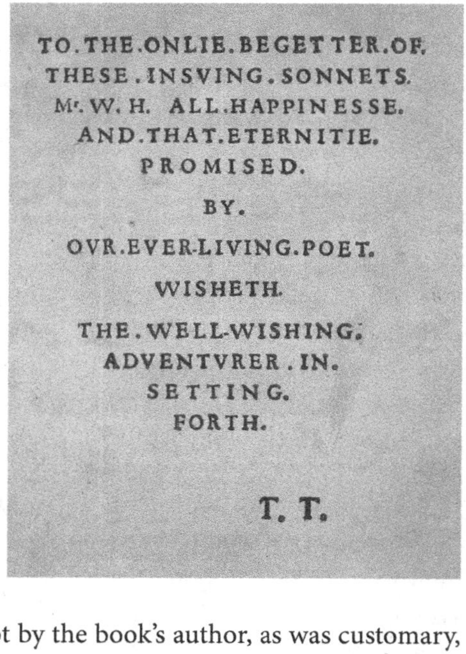

TO.THE.ONLIE.BEGETTER.OF.
THESE.INSVING.SONNETS.
Mr. W. H. ALL.HAPPINESSE.
AND.THAT.ETERNITIE.
PROMISED.

BY.

OVR.EVER-LIVING.POET.

WISHETH.

THE.WELL-WISHING.
ADVENTVRER.IN.
SETTING.
FORTH.

T. T.

Fig. 4.1 Dedication page, *Shake-speares Sonnets* (1609).

The dedication is signed not by the book's author, as was customary, and as Shakespeare himself had done in his two prior verse publications, *Venus and Adonis* and *Lucrece*. It is instead initialed by T. T., identified in the title-page imprint as the publisher Thomas Thorpe, whose practice it was to sign the dedications of works by authors long dead, like Lucan, Epictetus, and Augustine.[1] The dedication's reference to Shakespeare as "OUR.EVER.LIVING.POET" also seems to reference someone who while undying in fame or memory is already dead.[2] Even the beautiful ornamental headpiece on the title page has a mortuary aspect. Resembling a medallion frieze on an ancient sarcophagus, it consists of a plumed head at its center, enframed by putti, dolphins, rabbits, and acanthus—all Roman symbols of immortality (Fig. 4.2).

Fig. 4.2 Title page, ornamental header, *Shake-speares Sonnets* (1609).

From the vantage of the quarto's epitaphic threshold, the reader might be predisposed to see the rough quadrilaterals of fourteen-line poems as so many ledger slabs or gravestones, inscribed with lettering for posterity to scan.

Might the idea of printing the Sonnets as a posthumous work have issued from the sonnets themselves? In a number of them, as will be discussed below, the poet not only calls for death but imagines himself dead, buried, decomposing, and covered with dust. Thorpe has certainly read the Sonnets; indeed, he draws from them his wish for the dedicatee's prosperity, extending to Mr. W. H., "THAT.ETERNITIE.PROMISED.BY.OUR.EVER.LIVING.POET." Even this wish has a familiar graveside ring, echoing the promise of eternal life to the soul at the moment of the body's committal to earth.

In 1623 it was perfectly appropriate for the preliminaries to *Mr. William Shakespeares Comedies, Histories, & Tragedies* to present the volume as posthumous: the poet had predeceased the works whose survival the book was intended to secure. (For poets as for saints, death is the first step to canonization.) But for the dedication to the quarto to do so in 1609, when Shakespeare was alive and active, seems oddly premature. Why intimate what had not yet occurred?

As it happened, what was well-wishing in 1609 would in time prove true. Shakespeare would be dead and the Sonnets would endure. Now, more than 400 years after their publication, with the regular appearance of new editions and critical works, it seems safe to say that the Sonnets are well on their way to attaining their promised perpetuity that will extend if not "beyond all date even to eternity" (sonnet 122), then at least to the foreseeable future.[3]

***

Despite the combined efforts of the poet's verse and the publisher's press, Shakespeare's 1609 Sonnets almost perished. Far from being everlasting, the work proved short-lived, and exceptionally so. As Lukas Erne and Tamsin Badcoe have demonstrated, it is the only Shakespearean quarto not to be reprinted within twenty-five years of its publication, either as quarto or in the 1623 Folio of Shakespeare's dramatic works.[4] Even the other verse collection attributed to Shakespeare, *The Passionate Pilgrime,* was reprinted twice, in 1599 and 1612.

Scholars have been hard pressed to explain the 1609 Sonnets' early demise. It has often been attributed to the outmodedness of the sonnet form, but as Erne and Badcoe also note, sonnets were being reprinted long after 1609: Spenser's *Amoretti* in 1617, Daniel's *Delia* in 1623, and Drayton's *Idea* in 1637. Whatever the cause, it is ironic that the one work by Shakespeare that asserts its own perpetuity proved for a century to be his most ephemeral.

Not until over a century after its publication was the 1609 *Shakespeares Sonnets* reprinted, as the second volume of Bernard Lintott's *A Collection of Poems, in Two Volumes* (1711).[5] The first volume of the collection, published in 1709, consisted of four discrete verse publications attributed to Shakespeare, each with its own dated divisional title page: *Venus and Adonis* (1630), *The Rape of Lucrece* (1632), *The*

Passionate Pilgrime (1599), and *Sonnets to Sundry Notes of Musick* (1599).[6] In 1711, Lintott added a second volume reproducing Thorpe's 1609 *Sonnets*, described on its title page as "One Hundred and Fifty Four Sonnets, all of them in Praise of his Mistress" (rather imprecisely, since they are neither all to a mistress nor all praising). When conjoined, the two octavo volumes formed a single bibliographic unit comprising what its subtitle identifies as "*all the Miscellanies of Mr. William Shakespeare.*"

In reproducing the five "miscellanies" of his *A Collection of Poems*, Lintott attempted to replicate the typography of the early editions themselves. The 1711 title page claims that its content had been "Publish'd by [Shakespeare] himself in the Year 1609, and now correctly Printed from those Editions." The dates, 1630, 1632, 1599, 1599 and 1609" now appears on the divisional title page for each of the five units. Only in his newspaper and bookseller advertisements does Lintott explain that his collection was not of original quartos but instead had been "[p]rinted Literatim from those Editions." By "Literatim," Lintott does not mean "verbatim"—he means letter-by-letter, for the collection preserves not only the orthography of the 1609 *Sonnets* but its typography: "I have printed [the miscellanies] from very old Editions."[7] The 1711 composite is devised to look like a sammelband or multibook collection from the previous century.[8] Replicating the early print editions as closely as eighteenth-century print technology allowed,[9] it was designed to appeal to literary antiquarians like Lewis Theobald, Thomas Percy, and Edward Capell, who were engaged in the project of establishing a vernacular literary tradition through the recovery of old English texts. In his copy of Lintott's composite volume now held at Trinity College, Cambridge, Capell has corrected and modernized the text throughout all five "miscellanies," suggesting an intention to publish Thorpe's 1609 *Sonnets* not as a discrete work, as is often assumed, but as one of five Shakespearean miscellanies.[10]

Half a century after Lintott, the 1609 quarto was reprinted for a second time, again in combination with other works attributed to Shakespeare, this time not poetic miscellanies but play quartos. In 1766, George Steevens published in four volumes *Twenty of the Plays of Shakespeare: Being the whole number printed in quarto during his life-time, or before the Restoration.* The penultimate of those twenty quartos (followed by

the anonymous *The history of King Leir and his three daughters* [1605])
is a quarto not of a play but of the 1609 *Shake-speares Sonnets*. In the
advertisement to the four volumes, Steevens explains that he has collected the twenty quarto "pamphlets" into bound volumes in order to
"multiply the chances of their being preserved."[11] They are, he believes,
early drafts of plays, "the poet's first thoughts as well as words" which
would appear in their final form in the 1623 Folio. He makes no claim for
their literary value; indeed, he fears that their inferiority to the received
Folio versions risks damaging Shakespeare's reputation. Yet they are
important as historical records: "The general interest of ENGLISH literature, and the attention due to our own language and history, require
that our ancient writings should be diligently reviewed."[12] Shakespeare's
quartos are among the "ancient repositories" from which obsolete words
and phrases can be retrieved to the benefit of both the history of the
language and the understanding of its literature. He hopes their publication will incite "the extension and continuance" of the study of "the
old English writers" begun earlier in his century with the groundbreaking work on Anglo-Saxon of the linguist George Hickes.[13] If achieved,
Steevens hopes, England would have a history of its language and its
literature spanning from the Conquest to the Restoration.

When editing his own edition of Shakespeare in 1793, however,
Steevens denounces the Sonnets he had hoped in 1766 to rescue from
obscurity. His condemnation seems quite gratuitous, for surely an edition entitled *The Plays of William Shakspeare* need not apologize for
having excluded the poetry. Yet he defends their omission: "We have not
reprinted the Sonnets, &c. of Shakspeare because the strongest Act of
Parliament that could be framed would fail to compel readers into their
service."[14] This is ridiculous, of course: Parliament in his day might sup-
press books but not mandate their reading. One wonders if that isn't
what Steevens would have liked to say outright: that Parliament should
ban the Sonnets. And yet he himself had twenty-five years earlier taken it
upon himself to secure their survival. What accounts for the about-face?

It may well have been Malone's edition of 1780. It was one thing to
reproduce the Sonnets in their original 1609 form so that scholars might
seek out obsolete words and syntax, as Steevens had done in 1766. It was
quite another to modernize and annotate them for the appreciation of a

general readership and in the process to forge problematic connections to Shakespeare's life, as Malone did in 1780.

∗∗∗

In Malone's edition, the 1609 *Sonnets* was published for the first time as part of Shakespeare's dramatic corpus: first in 1780 as a supplement to *The Plays of William Shakspeare*, edited by Samuel Johnson and George Steevens (1778), then in Malone's own 1790 edition of *The Plays and Poems of William Shakspeare*, and finally in his posthumous 1821 edition of the same title, completed by James Boswell, Jr.[15] In the 1780 Supplement, Malone edited the Sonnets along with the seven "doubtful" plays that had been added to the third Shakespeare folio of 1664.[16] Their title-page attribution as well as their Stationers' Register entry was sufficient to establish their authenticity, as Malone allowed. In addition, most of the edition's notes, many provided by Steevens, consist of analogous passages from the dramatic works intended less to elucidate or emend the Sonnets than to suture them to the rest of the canon: "The numerous passages in [the Sonnets] which remind us of the authour's plays, leave not the smallest doubt of their authenticity" (217). The "ever-fixèd mark" of sonnet 116, for example, is used to link the sonnet to two plays: *King Henry VIII*, in which Wolsley compares his loyalty to the king to a rock that will "unshaken stand," and *Coriolanus*, in which the Roman general wishes his son to be steadfast in war like "the great sea mark, standing every flaw" (328–9 n. 1). Hundreds of such notes serve to fasten the 1609 *Sonnets* to the canon in advance of its incorporation into an edition of Shakespeare's works, volume 10 of Malone's 1790 *The Plays and Poems of William Shakspeare*.

But Malone wants to establish not only that Shakespeare wrote the Sonnets but that he wrote them about himself. From the start, he assumes that the first-person pronoun of the Sonnets designates the author named on the title page. As Shakespeare had embedded his own first name in the puns on "will" in sonnet 136, so Malone suspects he lodged Mr. W. H.'s surname in what he takes to be a pun in sonnet 20: "A man in hew all *Hews* in his controlling." "*Hews*," he explains, "was the old mode of spelling *hues* (colours), and also *Hughes*, the proper name" (242 n. 1). Edmund Spenser, Malone also surmises, is the rival poet or "better spirit" of sonnet 80, for he is the only contemporary poet who "at the zenith of his reputation" Shakespeare might have considered his superior (297 n. 9). The highpoint of Spenser's career coincides with the very early date Malone assigns to Shakespeare's writing of the Sonnets. He passes over the poet's several portrayals of himself as not only old but near death (sonnets 63 and 73, for example) and alights instead on what he takes to be allusions to Shakespeare's youth: "pupil pen" in sonnet 16 suggests that the sonnets are juvenilia, as does sonnet 32's self-deprecating reference to the immaturity of his verse: "We may hence, as well as from other circumstances, infer, that these were among our author's earliest compositions" (256 n. 1). Also corroborating an early dating is his literal reading of sonnet 23's opening simile: "As an unperfect actor on the stage / Who with his fear is put besides his part." Shakespeare, he infers, "had himself perhaps experienced" such stage fright when he first became "conversant with the stage" (245 n. 2). Also referencing his early acting career is sonnet 111's apology for having to rely on "public means which public manners breeds." As Malone observes, "the author seems to lament having been reduced to the necessity of appearing on the stage, or writing for the theatre" (323 n. 9).

Yet not all attributes are intended to be self-referential, Malone concedes, at least not literally so. When the poet is charged of "lameness" in sonnet 89, the expression is merely "figurative" (261, n.5). Nor is he to be thought "poor, nor despis'd," as he calls himself in sonnet 37, "for neither of which suppositions there is the smallest ground" (262 n. 5). Not so easily dismissed, however, is the implication of the division Malone imposes in his headnote to the Sonnets: "To this person [Mr. W.H.], whoever he was, one hundred and twenty six of the following poems are addressed; the remaining twenty-eight are addressed to a lady" (217). Shakespeare, already married and with children, it must be assumed, wrote love poems to a man and a mistress. These are the amatory relationships that alarm both his mentor, George Steevens, and his posthumous co-editor, James Boswell, Jr. Steevens, in the note he contributes to sonnet 20, is repelled by the poet's attraction to the sexually ambiguous "master-mistress of my passion": "I find it impossible to read without an equal mixture of disgust and indignation."[17] Yet Malone, as we have seen, apparently unfazed by the queer epithet, turns to this very sonnet for the identity of the "master-mistress," Mr. W.H. He attempts to temper Steevens's indignation by relativizing the sonnet's rhetoric: "such addresses to men, however indelicate, were customary in our author's time, and neither imported criminality, nor were esteemed indecorous" (241 n. 8).[18] Yet the contemporary analogue he supplies in annotating sonnet 20's notorious conceit suggests that such indelicacies are hardly bygone. He finds a "modern epigram" in which, as in Shakespeare's sonnet, Nature's last-minute addition of a prick or pin to the body she has fashioned makes all the difference:

> There is an odd coincidence between these lines and a
> well-known modern epigram:
> "Whilst nature Hervey's clay was blending,
> "Uncertain what the thing would end in,
> "Whether a female or a male,
> "A pin dropp'd in, and turn'd the scale. (242 n. 3)

While markedly reticent on the two illicit liaisons introduced by his own textual apparatus, in a note spanning five pages in reduced print Malone oddly belabors a relationship nowhere mentioned in the Sonnets.[19] The note is keyed to the first line and a half of sonnet 93: "So shall I live, supposing thou art true, / Like a deceivèd husband" (305–9 n. 4). Yet his note's pretext is not the sonnet, but rather William Oldys's observation on it, penned in his copy of Langbaine.[20] Oldys observed that sonnets 92 and 93 "seem to have been addressed by Shakespeare to his beautiful wife on some suspicion of her infidelity" (305).[21] Malone first summarily writes off the comment. Oldys had failed to observe what Malone's editorial directive would stress: none of the first 126 sonnets are addressed to "a female." All the same Malone defends Oldys's biographical conjecture with "circumstances" of varying evidentiary status—an anecdotal report, four plays, and finally and most decisively, a legal instrument—all brought forth to prove his case: that Shakespeare was the "deceivèd husband" of sonnet 93.

First there is "the well known story of the Oxford vintner's wife" who entertained Shakespeare on his stopovers between London and Stratford and with such intimacy that he was rumored to have fathered her son. By Malone's construal, the account bears witness to the infidelity not of Shakespeare but of his wife. His infidelity, he tacitly and speciously assumes, must have been provoked by hers. The same betrayal is implied, Malone insists, by the frequency and intensity with which jealousy is dramatized in the plays: "jealousy is the principle hinge of four of his plays." In them, "[Shakespeare] appears to me to have written more immediately *from the heart* on the subject of jealousy than on any other; and it is therefore not improbable he might have felt it" (306). He finds Othello's passionate outbursts particularly telling. The "exquisite feeling" they evince "might lead us to suspect that the author, at some period of his life, had himself been *perplexed* with doubts, though not perhaps *in the extreme*" (306). (The fact that the jealousy of all four husbands— Ford, Leontes, Posthumus and Othello—is ultimately exposed as folly or error gets no mention here.)

If Shakespeare's suspicion was not "*in the extreme*," it certainly was persistent, at least in Malone's mind.[22] By his construal, it remains with Shakespeare to his dying day, as evidenced by his will. He appoints his daughter rather than his wife as his executor and, more tellingly, bequeaths to his wife only "an old piece of furniture," and even that, Malone adds, in an interlinear afterthought. In a startlingly telepathic moment, Malone describes what ran through Shakespeare's mind as he lay on his deathbed:

> His wife had not wholly escaped his memory; he had forgot her,— he had recollected her,—but so recollected her, as more strongly to mark how little he esteemed her; he had already (as it is vulgarly expressed) cut her off, not indeed with a shilling, but with an old bed. (308–9)

This single sentence does more than describe how Shakespeare felt. Its stressed syntactic breaks simulate jealousy's rupturing psychic effect. Indeed Malone edits Othello's breakdown before his collapse into "a trance" with similarly heavy interpunction, including the rare combination of em dash after another punctuation mark.[23]

Lie with her! lie; on her!—We say, lie on her, when they belie
her: Lie with her! that's fulsome.—Handkerchief,—confessions,—
handkerchief.—To confess, and be hanged for this labour. I tremble at
it.[24]

Malone invoking Shakespeare as he lay drying, syntactically enacts the
agitation he supposes him to have felt while executing his will. His
sentence culminates, as does Othello's paroxysm, with the desire for
revenge: he resolves to take if not his wife's life ("I will chop her into
messes!") then at least her means of livelihood ("cut her off, not indeed
with a shilling"). Malone, we might say, throws himself into what he
takes to be Shakespeare's experience, performing on the page the passion
he believes the playwright suffered throughout his adult life. Like the taking of Shakespeare's signature discussed at the beginning of Chapter 3,
the reenactment of his deathbed sentiments draws him closer to Shakespeare. As Steevens had traced the palsied motions of Shakespeare's
hand on his last will and testament, so Malone entertains the torturous
thoughts that by his projection racked Shakespeare's mind.

It is not sonnet 93 that called for Malone's extravagant and extra-
neous note, but rather Malone's determination to read the Sonnets
autobiographically. The subject of Shakespeare's marriage allows him to
shift focus from the extramarital to the marital. In addition, the back
story he invents of Shakespeare's wife's betrayal goes some way toward
mitigating the breach of wedlock entailed by a biographical reading.
Better to cast Shakespeare as the offended and retaliating "jealous husband," even the derisory cuckold, than as the offending sodomite or
adulterer.

Alarmed, perhaps, by Malone's scholarly abandon, Steevens interjects
a note setting strict limits on biographical inquiry:

[A]ll that is known with any degree of certainty concerning Shakspeare, is—that he was born at Stratford upon Avon,—married and
had children there,—went to London, where he commenced actor,
and wrote poems and plays,—returned to Stratford, made his will, died,
and was buried. (306)

He rejects Malone's evidence: Shakespeare might have made provisions for his wife elsewhere;[25] the will's interlineations were perhaps the result of illness; only in *Othello* is jealousy "the principal hinge."[26] He objects to the critical assumption that expressions of heightened emotion in his characters are revelatory of what Shakespeare's himself experienced. By the same logic, Steevens argues, Shakespeare would have suffered the "filial ingratitude" of Lear or the murderous depravity of Macbeth or the cynicism and misanthropy of Appematus and Timon. "Are we to suppose," Steevens asks, that Shakespeare copied the "vindictive cruelty of Shylock ... from a fiend-like original in his own bosom?" (307). Or, we might add, that the notorious "master-mistress" of sonnet 20 was the object of Shakespeare's passion?

In his outsized note to sonnet 93, Malone repeatedly allows that his biographical query is "pure conjecture." Yet he hammers it out on three other occasions: in his manuscript notes to Langbaine, his annotations to Shakespeare's will and in his exposure of Ireland's forgeries.[27] While later editors of the Sonnets drop Malone's conjectural note on sonnet 93, it is picked up by later biographers. As early as 1832, the allegation surfaces in Alexander Dyce's "Memoir of Shakespeare": "From some of Shakespeare's Sonnets, it has been supposed that, after [Shakespeare] became a husband, he was by no means remarkable for purity of morals."[28] He cites as his authority Malone's note to sonnet 93.[29]

In his "Preliminary Remarks" to the Sonnets in the 1821 edition, Boswell joins forces with Steevens against Malone's "uncomfortable conjecture" (309 n. 4). Indeed he openly challenges his mentor's premises. In his first note to Malone's edition, Boswell scotches Malone's identification of Mr. W. H as the addressee of the Sonnets: Mr. W. H. is "merely the person who *gets* or *procures*" the manuscript and delivers it to the publisher. So, too, Boswell pronounces all of Malone's other "personal connections" null and void. Malone believed sonnet 111 to be Shakespeare's remonstrance against his theatrical profession. No such complaint, insists Boswell, could have issued from Shakespeare, to whom the theatre had brought fame and fortune. But a more important principle is at stake. If any one detail were taken as self-referential, all would have to be. That would make Shakespeare the perpetrator of "harmful deeds" whose "name receives a brand" and whose brow is stamped by "vulgar scandal" (111). To admit one "personal connection" was to open the floodgates to them all:

> If Shakspeare was speaking of himself [in sonnet 111], it would follow that he is equally pointed at upon other occasions, so he must also have been grossly and notoriously profligate. To say nothing of the criminal connection, (for criminal in a high degree it would certainly have been in a married man,) which is frequently alluded to in those Sonnets which are said to be addressed by him in his own character to a female. (220)

Criminal to an even higher degree, must have assumes, would have been those "addressed by him in his own character" to a male.[30]

While the Shakespeare of the anecdotes discussed in Chapter 1 was characterized by "harmful deeds"—adultery, theft, libel, treason, and blasphemy—Boswell's Shakespeare is categorically beyond reproach: "We may lament that we know so little of his history; but this, at least, may be asserted with confidence, that at no time was the slightest imputation cast upon his moral character" (220). By Boswell's circular logic, Shakespeare was in all respects reputable; the "I" of the Sonnets is disreputable; therefore, the "I" of the Sonnets cannot be Shakespeare. Malone's assumption, he concludes, is just plain wrong: "The man depicted in the Sonnets could not be put for gentle Shakspeare." Rather than impute wrongdoing to Shakespeare, he rejects all biographical inferences and thereby overthrows his mentor's foundational premise. The Sonnets he maintains, are nothing but "effusions of fancy," written for the amusement of Shakespeare's friends.

Four decades after the publication of the first critical edition of the 1609 Sonnets in 1780, Boswell regretfully concedes that Malone's first-person reading has prevailed: "it seems to have been generally admitted that the poet speaks in his own person" (219).[31] Despite his and Steevens's attempts to quell the "personal connections," they take hold. William Wordsworth's description of the Sonnets in a critical essay as "poems, in which Shakespeare expresses his own feelings in his own person" closely echoes Malone's edition, whose notes he knew.[32] To read the Sonnets is to be privy to Shakespeare's innermost being: "with this same key Shakespeare unlocked his heart."[33] By the end of the same century, Edward Dowden, in his own edition of the Sonnets (1881), lists the authorities who read the Sonnets as Malone's edition prescribed, himself included:

> With Wordsworth, Sir Henry Taylor, and Mr. Swinburne, with François-Victor Hugo, with Kreyſſig, Ulrici, Gervinus, and Hermann Iſaac, with Boaden, Armitage Brown, and Hallam, with Furnival, Spalding, Rossetti, and Palgrave, I believe that Shakspere's Sonnets express his own feelings in his own person.[34]

Unmediated by the characters of his plays or the impersonal narrator of the narrative poems, their unique promise of access to Shakespeare's person proved irresistible, despite its problematic implications.

One commentator wrote just a decade too late to make Dowden's list: the novelist, critic, and classicist Samuel Butler. His *Shakespeare's Sonnets Reconsidered* (1899) is an accomplished reading of the Sonnets as an autobiographical narrative precisely situated in time. As Butler admits from the start, having recently translated Homer, he has no qualms about acknowledging Shakespeare's love for a man.[35] Indeed, for Butler, that love becomes the sole subject of all the Sonnets; the mistress the two men share serves only to strengthen the bond between them. Ignoring Malone's division after sonnet 126, he assigns all the sonnets not explicitly addressed to a female to the male lover; the remaining ones to the mistress, he proposes, were written for his lover to send to the mistress they shared.

Most remarkable is Butler's rearrangement of all but eight of the sonnets to follow what he proposes as the chronological order: the order in which the events occurred and in which the sonnets recording them were written.[36] On the basis of internal references alone, he dates each sonnet by month and year along the three-year duration, from 1583 to 1586, commemorated in sonnet 104 ("Three winters' cold ... three summers' pride, / Three beauteous springs"), extending from the first sight of his lover ("when first your eye I eyed") to his taking leave of him ("Farewell, thou art too dear for my possessing" [sonnet 87]). That the chronological narrative was not previously self-evident, he maintains, was the fault of the publisher's having scrambled the order Shakespeare had intended. So confident is Butler of having ascertained that order that he prints the Sonnets in his rearrangement and in facsimile type pieces, some of which, he explains, had been made expressly for the purpose, so that his edition would look just as it should have in 1609, had the publisher been faithful to Shakespeare's manuscript.

With his commentary and edition of the Sonnets, Butler could be said to have achieved what Malone had attempted in his Life of Shakespeare. He situated both Shakespeare's works and his life on the same continuous timeline, with periodic dated entries, like those in a diary, simultaneously marking the time of the event and its rendering in verse. Like Ireland's forgeries discussed in Chapter 3, Butler's reconstituted Sonnets might be seen as a materialization of Malone's impossible longings, in this instance for Shakespeare's personal notebook: "I will not despair of finding Shakespeare's pocketbook."[37] It may have been Malone's inference from sonnets 77 and 122 that gave him cause to dream of such a find. In sonnet 77, the poet gives his friend a table-book of blank pages intended for the inscription of his thoughts: "thy mind's imprint will bear." The gift is reciprocated, as Malone notes: "We learn from the 122d Sonnet that Shakespeare received a *table-book* from his friend" (296 n. 3). Malone's interest in Shakespeare's personal papers might well have left him wondering, was there once a table-book that bore the imprint of Shakespeare's mind?

But a sixteenth- or seventeenth-century table-book is not the same as an eighteenth-century pocketbook. Malone may have been envisioning the portable notebook popular in his own time, consisting of paper pages written in pen and ink, containing personal memoranda, possibly dated.[38] Shakespeare's vademecum, had he owned one, would most likely have taken the form of the many table-books that have survived from the period.[39] Consisting of waxed pages, these tablets were to be inscribed with extracts from other writers and speakers; once transcribed for future use into a stationary manuscript book, they would have been wiped clean.

***

In the textual history of the Sonnets as sketched above, *Shake-speares Sonnets* (1609) was not reprinted until a century after its publication and then not with Shakespeare's dramatic corpus but in other collections: the first, a collection of miscellanies in 1711, the second, of quartos in 1766. The survival of the 1609 *Sonnets* was not secured until it was published as part of Shakespeare's canon, embedded in a critical apparatus that identified its first-person pronoun with Shakespeare and that proposed connections between the Sonnets and both Shakespeare's life and his works. Yet this account of the history of the Sonnets' publication has thus far ignored what both editors and critics regularly term "the second edition of Shakespeare's Sonnets": John Benson's 1640 *Poems: Written by Wil. Shake-speare. Gent.* Even in this century, editors continue to blame Benson for having deprived the world of the real article, the authentic 1609 *Shake-speares Sonnets*: "For well over a century Benson succeeded in muddying the waters … until the superb work of Edmund Malone in 1780."[40]

As a second edition of the 1609 *Sonnets*, Benson's *Poems* is indeed a mess.[41] It changes the 1609 title, replaces its preface, tacitly drops eight of the 154 sonnets, compresses the rest into a total of seventy-two poems by combining up to five sonnets, introduces as many as 759 textual variants,[42] scrambles the 1609 order, tacitly intersperses poems from other collections and by other poets, replaces the ordinal numbers with generic titles (some of which alter male pronouns to female), and inserts elegies on Shakespeare's death followed by an appendix of poems by later authors.[43] What could possibly explain such a travesty?

Criminal intent was long held to be the motive. Benson, it was supposed, had stolen the 1609 *Sonnets* and covered up the theft by overlaying titles and non-Shakespearean verses and conjoining as many as five sonnets to look like longer verse forms. Hyder E. Rollins's colorful account in the authoritative 1944 New Variorum edition of the Sonnets long proved irresistible: "Benson pirated Thorpe's [1609 quarto] text, but took such great pains to conceal his piracy that he has deceived many modern scholars, just as apparently he hoodwinked the wardens of the Stationers' Company." (By Rollins's logic, Benson would have expected buyers to have been more discerning than the Company officials, detecting the presence of the valued 1609 *Sonnets* beneath the 1640 muddle.) Having exposed what he supposes to be the fraudulent intent behind what he assumes to be a shamefully disfiguring reproduction of the 1609 *Sonnets*, Rollins regrets having to refer to the 1640 *Poems* as "a second edition of the Sonnets."[44] He is right to have qualms, but not because it is such a bad edition of Shakespeare's 1609 *Sonnets*.

Should a text be considered an edition of a work from which it deviates so radically? The verses included in the 1640 *Poems* are drawn from five other printed sources besides the 1609 *Sonnets*: *Englands Helicon* (1614); *Loves Martyr* (1603, 1611); *Troia Britannica* (1609); *The Passionate Pilgrime* (1612); and two songs from Shakespeare's plays. Why, then, should the 1640 *Poems* be considered a second edition of the 1609 *Sonnets* instead of, say, the fourth edition of William Jaggard's *The Passionate Pilgrime* (1612)? Benson printed the latter, unlike the former, in its entirety; in the case of the two sonnets that are printed in both collections, Benson favors *The Passionate Pilgrime* text.[45] He follows Jaggard's principle of selection, assembling all the poems that might pass for Shakespeare's and that were not the property of other publishers. Like Jaggard, too, Benson forgoes the uniformity of the 1609 quarto's 154 sonnets in favor of poems of diverse lengths and kinds. Unlike *Shake-speares Sonnets*, *The Passionate Pilgrime*, having gone through four reprints by 1640, had proven its vendibility.

Benson's 1640 *Poems: Written by Wil. Shake-speare. Gent.* is no more a second edition of Thorpe's 1609 *Shake-speares Sonnets* than of Jaggard's *The Passionate Pilgrime*. It is instead the first edition of a compilation of poems of various lengths and topics, drawn from other collections and publications, which also includes most of the 1609 *Sonnets*, many in composite form. Depending on the copy, elegies on Shakespeare are placed either before or after the poems assigned to Shakespeare, or in some cases at both ends, all correctly attributed. (The single anonymous poem remains unidentified.) Benson further enriched the collection by adding previously unpublished poems by later authors in a separate section sharply differentiated by title: "An addition of some excellent poems, to those precedent, of renowned Shakespeare, by other gentlemen." Benson went to the further labor of grouping those sonnets together that he thought shared a subject or occasion and of giving them a descriptive title. He thereby produced a new bibliographic unit from that of any of the collections he drew from and one that belongs to another print genre from the Sonnets altogether. The 1640 *Poems* is not a sonnet collection in the tradition of the English sonneteers inaugurated by Philip Sidney's *Astrophil and Stella* (1591) but an anthology or compilation popular from the time of Richard Tottel's groundbreaking *Songes and Sonnettes* (1557), now known as *Tottel's Miscellany*.[46]

Benson, as has been demonstrated, was doing nothing illegal or even irregular in publishing the 1640 *Poems*.[47] The owner of the 1609 quarto copyright, Thomas Thorpe, had died in 1635 without having transferred his right to the work. The copyright, it is now granted, had lapsed and reverted to the Stationers' Company. But if Benson's *Poems* is a work in its own right, can the status of Thorpe's copyright be the issue? In the next century, when editions of the 1609 *Sonnets* and the 1640 *Poems* were prepared for publication within a year of one another (1710/11) by Bernard Lintott and Charles Gildon, respectively, both texts were licensed.[48] Colin Burrow points out what appears to have previously gone unnoticed: "For copyright purposes it seems likely that Gildon's volume could count as a different work from Lintott's."[49] There is no conflict over the copyright because the stationers recognize two discrete texts.

Benson has modeled his octavo of diverse poems on the 1623 Folio's collection of multi-genre plays. Like the Folio's compilers, John Heminges and Henry Condell, he appointed himself custodian of the scattered works, in the hope that they would attain "proportionale glory, with the rest of his *everliving Workes*."[50] As in the Folio, the emphasis is on Shakespeare's decease (see Chapter 1). Two elegies open the volume, "Upon Master WILLIAM SHAKESPEARE, the Deceased Authour, and his POEMS" by Leonard Digges and "Of Mr. William Shakespeare" by John Warren. Three memorial verses close off the poems attributed to Shakesepeare: "An Epitaph on the admirable Dramaticke Poet, William Shakespeare," by [I.M.] John Milton; "On the death of William Shakespeare, who died in Aprill, Anno Dom. 1616" by [W.B.] William Basse; and "An Elegie on the death of that famous Writer and Actor, M. William Shakspeare," unattributed. The frontispiece effigy is a reversed and reduced copy of the Folio's Droeshout engraving, now looking even more ghostly with the insertion of a sepulchral ledge before the effigy and a mysterious aureole behind its head. In the 1623 Folio, the effigy is called a "figure"; here it is termed a "shadow" (Fig. 1.4).

As with the Folio's gathering of Shakespeare's dramatic remains, this compilation of his poetic ones is a postmortem project. In his prefatory elegy to the *Poems*, John Warren likens Benson's collection and reconstitution of Shakespeare's scattered poetic remains to Asclepius' reassembling of Hippolytus' dismembered body; in both cases, the outcome is another corpus: "What, lofty *Shakespeare*, art againe reviv'd? / And *Virbius* like now show'st thy selfe twise liv'd." In the last book of Ovid's *Metamorphoses*, Hippolytus, having been mangled to death in a chariot race, is brought back to life by Asclepius—but as another man, Virbius, who will live out his days as one of the lesser gods in the precinct of Diana.[51]

***

Once Benson's 1640 *Poems* ceases to be identified as an irresponsible "second edition" of the 1609 *Shake-speares Sonnets*, it can be appreciated for what it is. As a number of recent scholars have demonstrated, it is a miscellany of poems drawn from several different sources, gathered together and formatted for the convenience of the reader. The features deplorable to later editors would have been perfectly familiar to Benson's readers: the conjoining of verses, casual attributions, regendering of pronouns, indifference to source context, and, most notably, the insertion of headings. As Jean-Christophe Mayer observes:

> The editor of the 1640 *Poems* was really only transferring to the sphere of print practices that were entirely normal in the manuscript world. Not only were these practices customary, but they were some of the

ways in which Shakespeare's words came to be disseminated and exchanged through the scribal medium.[52]

Benson was not only observing manuscript practices: he was facilitating their continuation. His *Poems* formed a printed platform inviting the extraction of its content. Jason Scott-Warren nicely describes how the practice of reading poetic texts was not an end in itself: rather, it was the start of a process that consisted of the marking of a select passage, its transcription, classification, storage, retrieval, and finally its redeployment in speech or writing.[53] The features excoriated by later editors would have constituted the very attractions of the 1640 *Poems* for early readers. Instead of 154 uniform amatory sonnets, it delivered poems of varying lengths and subjects, all either by Shakespeare or associated with him in print, and supplemented them with a separately titled addition of fifteen more recent and fashionable poems of his poetic successors.[54]

To have all these poems in one volume spared readers what for most would have been the insurmountable challenge of obtaining access to three separate printed volumes of verse. The poems in "An addition ... by other gentlemen" would have been all but impossible to come by; before Benson, they existed only in manuscript. Adding to the variety were the five elegiac tributes encasing the Shakespearean poems. Benson did the reader a further service by giving descriptive titles to poems that had previously been published without titles or, in the case of Shakespeare's Sonnets, with only numerals. In sum, Benson produced an octavo small enough to be pocketed, containing a rich and varied collection of poems culled from disparate printed and manuscript sources, grouped and titled to facilitate their subsequent organization under topics.

No feature of Benson's edition has been more heavily criticized than his insertion of titles. Yet earlier readers would have seen them not as contentious interventions but as helpful directives, like headnotes that provide a point of entry to what they precede. The titles would have served to facilitate commonplacing. Benson's title for sonnet 121, "Errour in Opinion," doesn't begin to cover the ethical and epistemological complexities of a sonnet whose first line is "'Tis better to be vile than vile esteemèd," but it does suggest a possible topic heading and invite alternatives like "Reputation," "Slander," or "A Good Name."[55] Benson's grouping of five sonnets (60, 63, 64, 65, 66) under the rubric "Injurious Time" promises a miniature storehouse of topoi on that subject. Three of his titles are themselves Latin tags, readily commonplaced. Sonnet 62's "*Sat fuisse*" might fall under such rubrics as "Sufficiency" or "Plenty"; sonnet 70's "*Nil Magnis Invidia*" under "Envy" or "Greatness"; and sonnet 61's "*Patiens Armatus*" under "Patience" or "Suffering."

Other titles speak to a more modern literary sensibility. Benson groups sonnets 71, 72, and 74 under the title "A Valediction," a term Donne had recently anglicized to refer both to death and to less permanent leave-takings.[56] Sonnet 22 ("My glass shall not persuade me I am old") is titled "A conceit," acknowledging the familiar Petrarchan conceit of the exchange of hearts on which the sonnet pivots, while also hinting at the word's recently acquired sense of self-infatuation. The meaning of "A Master-peece," the title Benson gives sonnet 24 in reference to the portrait hanging in the poet's bosom, had only recently been extended from a work which qualified a craftsman for guild membership to a consummate aesthetic achievement.

Benson's assignment of titles merely follows and promotes the reading practices that early readers had already been applying to the Sonnets when transcribing them. Of the twelve sonnets quoted in manuscripts (in whole or in part) from the 1609 quarto, six have been given descriptive titles.[57] The most frequently transcribed of the poems, sonnet 2 ("When forty winters shall besiege thy brow"), received several different titles. Two transcribers quite reasonably take the addressee who is being urged to beget a "fair child" to be a woman and title their transcriptions accordingly: "A Lover to his Mistress" and "To one yt wold dye a Mayd," the latter title drawing out the sonnet's *carpe diem* strain.[58] Another transcriber devises the title "Benefitt of Mariage," echoing Thomas Wilson's translation of the sonnet's Erasmian source, "An epistle to persuade a young Gentleman to marriage," which Wilson included in his *The Arte of Rhetorique* (1553). The most literary of the rubrics appears in three manuscripts: "Spes Altera," the epithet that Virgil in the last book of the *Aeneid* applies to Rome's next hope after Aeneas, his son Ascanius.[59] In keeping with this practice, Benson proposes still another title for his composite of sonnets 1 to 3, "Loves Crueltie," foregrounding what all three sonnets blame in the addressee: his or her self-absorbed refusal to give the world the "fair child" that is its due. What could be more cruel than the desire "to stop posterity" (sonnet 3)?

Benson's own printed text was in due course subject to the same practices he had applied to the poems he compiled.[60] Indeed, readers' marks in copies of the 1640 *Poems* bear witness to his success in encouraging the continuation of its own formatted practices. As Sasha Roberts first observed, owners of Benson's *Poems* took the option of altering his titles, not only in manuscript transcriptions of verses from the 1640 *Poems* but in printed copies of the book itself.[61] One reader, for example, crosses out Benson's title for sonnet 138, "False Belief," and replaces it with "Mutual Flattery" to foreground what is stressed by the sonnet's couplet: the gratifying complicity between the poet and his mistress. So, too, the reader of sonnet 53, "What is your substance, whereof are you made," changes Benson's "True Admiration" to the more philosophically charged and phonetically catchy "Imitability and Immutability," a tight paraphrase of the praise of the sonnet's couplet: "In all external grace you have some part, / But you like none, none you, for constant heart."[62]

Insofar as the poems of the 1609 quarto circulate in the second half of the seventeenth century, in both manuscript and print, it is in Benson's miscellany. While it was not reprinted in the seventeenth century, the 1658 *Catalogue of the Most Vendible books in England* includes Benson's 1640 *Poems*.[63] Manuscript miscellanies after 1640 are quoting Shakespeare's sonnets in whole or part from the 1640 *Poems*.[64] So, too, two compilers of printed poetic miscellanies, Edward Phillips (1656) and Joshua Poole (1658), reproduce sonnets from Benson. Even John Suckling, it has recently been demonstrated, draws on Benson's edition rather than Thorpe's for the extensive quotation from the Sonnets in his play *Brennoralt*.[65] When the poems for the first time are added to an edition of Shakespeare's plays—in Gildon's 1710 seventh volume to Rowe's six of 1709)—*Venus and Adonis* and *Lucrece* are followed by the content of Benson's 1640 *Poems: Written by Wil. Shake-speare. Gent.*, without Benson's obviously non-Shakespearean appendix and elegies.[66] Editions of Shakespeare continue to include Benson's 1640 *Poems* up to John Bell's edition of Shakespeare in 1804. The 1609 *Sonnets*, however, as we have seen, is not affixed to the canon until Malone's 1780 *Supplement* and not properly incorporated until his 1790 edition of *The Plays and Poems*.[67]

For almost a century and a half, then, Shakespeare's Sonnets were read in a miscellany that precluded autobiographical readings. They circulated without the dedication to Mr. W. H., later identified as the addressee of sonnets 1–126, and indeed without the divisional sonnet 126, one of the eight sonnets Benson had, perhaps inadvertently, omitted. The first person was generic, inclusive rather than individuated. Titles, thematic groupings, the reordered sequence, the interspersal of poems from other collections: all obviated the possibility of any kind of biographical reading. Nor is there any sure sign that the Sonnets were read as written in Shakespeare's own person before 1640. Nowhere is there evidence of readers searching for particulars relating to Shakespeare: his sexual proclivities, his profession, his poetic rivalry, his gait, his riding on horseback, his possession of a table-book, or his extramarital affairs. Gildon ventures that Shakespeare's mistress had possession of the 1640 poems before consigning them to her executor, but only to explain a publication date so long after Shakespeare's decease.[68] If readers were interested in the thoughts and feelings expressed in the Sonnets, it would have been insofar as they qualified as topics or commonplaces: general truths whose succinct and self-contained formulation allowed for easy lifting and redeployment.

***

Within a year of Lintott's publication of the 1609 *Sonnets* in *A Collection of Poems in Two Volumes* (1711), Gildon's second edition of Benson's 1640 *Poems* appeared. Published as a supplement to Nicholas Rowe's 1709 edition of Shakespeare, it contained Shakespeare's two narrative poems, but instead of the 1609 *Shake-speares Sonnets*, it reproduced the 1640 *Poems* (minus the patently non-Shakespeaean materials), retitling the collection *Mr. Shakespear's Miscellany Poems*. That both volumes should have appeared just after the publication of the first eighteenth-century edition of Shakespeare, Rowe's *The Works of Mr. William Shakespear* (1709), was no coincidence.[69] Both volumes were intended as sequels to this edition. At the very close of his *Some Account of the Life,*

& c., Rowe had left an opening for such an addition: he mentions having "encountered a Book of Poems, publish'd in 1640, under the Name of Mr. William Shakespear," but refrains from venturing "whether it be his or no."[70]

Both Lintott and Gildon, through opposite strategies of self-presentation, design their editions to look as if they "be his." The title page to Lintott's 1711 edition claims that the contents "were publish'd by [Shakespeare] himself in the year 1609, and now correctly Printed from those Editions," and omits the eighteenth-century date of the volume's actual publication. Most remarkably, as we have seen, Lintott's edition authenticates itself by simulating the spelling, typography, and ornamentation of the early quartos and octavos. Gildon and his publisher take the opposite tack, modeling their edition of the 1640 *Poems* not on the old 1609 quarto but on Rowe's recent 1709 six-volume octavo edition. "Printed on the same Paper and Letter as the six Volumes of Plays lately publish'd,"[71] it looked close enough to Rowe's six volumes to be added as the seventh to the set. By 1714, his volume was published as part of Rowe's edition proper. Until Malone in 1780, if editions of Shakespeare include his sonnets, they derive from the 1640 *Poems*, not the 1609 *Sonnets*.

Thus, Shakespeare's Sonnets, insofar as they attained the perpetuity they arrogate to themselves, did so after 1640 and into the eighteenth century in the form not of the 1609 quarto but of the 1640 octavo. For almost a century and a half, they were read in a miscellany format with impersonal generic titles that precluded the very feature by which Shakespeare's 1609 *Sonnets* was, as we have seen, belatedly admitted into the canon: the identification of the first person with Shakespeare. Lintott's sammelband, which included the 1609 *Sonnets*, was never incorporated into the canon.[72] By contrast, editions of Benson's 1640 *Poems* were reproduced fourteen times in the eighteenth century, either in editions of Shakespeare's works or independently.[73]

In addition to replicating the look of Rowe's edition, Gildon also promoted his publisher Jacob Tonson's project of elevating Shakespeare's vernacular drama to the ranks of the ancients (see Chapter 1 and Fig. 1.5). His seventh volume containing Benson's *Poems* includes a two-hundred-page essay, "Critical Remarks on his Plays, & c.," in which he discusses every play in Rowe's six-volume edition as well as the two narrative poems in his own seventh volume, defining the dramatic genres and repeatedly putting Shakespeare in relation to his ancient precedents. If Shakespeare fell short of them, Gildon maintains, how superior to them he would have been had his native talent been directed by their models: "He would have been the *Sophocles* of *England*, as he is now little more than the *Thespis*, or at most the *Aeschylus*."[74] While Gildon does not discuss the individual poems from the miscellany, he does identify the bulk of them with the genre of Martial and Catullus: "All that I have to say of the Miscellaneous Poems, is, that they are generally Epigrams and those perfect in their kind, according to the best rules that have been drawn from the Practices of the ancients."[75] His lengthy exposition of those rules includes a succinct definition of the genre: "All things are the allow'd Subject of the Epigram; as long as they are treated of with Brevity, Point, and Beauty." Gildon ends his long essay abruptly, without applying the rules he has laid down to the poems themselves. The essay, he explains, has already exceeded its bounds. He thereby leaves to the reader the impossible task of bringing generic precedents to bear on the poems of a *miscellany*, a mix-up of poetic kinds.

There is one form, however, in which Shakespeare, according to Gildon, unqualifiedly outdid the ancients: "But it is no small Honour to him, that he has surpass'd [the Ancients] in the Topics or Common Places."[76] Rather than plots or characters, his distinction lies in "[h]is surprizing Reflections and Topics ... for in these no Man ever excelled him."[77] Throughout the essay, Gildon culls topoi from each of the plays and narrative poems, highlighting them with italics. At the conclusion of his essay, he supplies an appendix, "References to the Classic Authors, & c.," consisting of some thirty topic headings, each one followed by references to topoi first from Shakespeare and then from a cluster of ancient authors, so that the reader can observe how Shakespeare's topoi "answer those [Topics], which have been touch'd on by the *Ancients*."[78] (He also tacks on a list of "Topics of Shakespeare for which I have not met with Parallels among the Latins.") While he provides no parallels from the *Miscellany Poems*, he does give readers the means to do so. The "Table" that follows the essay lists the titles Benson had assigned to the miscellany in 1640, the majority of which, as we have seen, are themselves topoi. With this aid, the reader might easily find analogues in the preceding table of "Reference to the Classical Authors." For example, the sonnet composite Benson has named "Glory of Beauty" (sonnets 67 to 69) might be matched with the references under the heading "Beauty" that include passages in Virgil, Ovid, Horace, Statius, Lucretius, etc.; so, too, if "Injurious Time" (sonnets 60, 63–66 in Benson/Gildon) were of interest, the heading "Time" would yield parallel passages in Ovid, Ausonius, Claudian, Seneca, etc. To affix the 1640 *Poems* to Shakespeare's corpus, Gildon linked them not to Shakespeare's other works and life, as Malone in 1780 would do with the 1609 *Sonnets,* but by demonstrating their affiliation with the same classical resources as the plays.

In the preface to his edition of Shakespeare (1765), Samuel Johnson also commends Shakespeare for his formulation of general truths, the result not of his book learning but of his own lived experience: "a vigilance of observation and accuracy of distinction which books and precepts cannot confer."[79] As a result, Johnson estimates, Shakespeare may have provided more maxims than all succeeding English writers combined: "it may be doubted, whether from all his successors more maxims of theoretical knowledge, or more rules of practical prudence, can be collected, than he alone has given to his country."[80] Having compiled his formidable 1755 *Dictionary*, Johnson had the authority to make such a generalization. His *Dictionary* subjoins each definition with quotations "taken from the best writers" in English: 1,000 of them are drawn from Shakespeare, more than from any other single author, exceeded only by the King James Bible, and many of them have the semantic self-sufficiency of topoi or maxims. If, as he claims in his preface, Johnson relied on his memory for the quotations, he had more lines of Shakespeare in mind than of any other author. For readers who consulted his *Dictionary*, Shakespeare's lines exemplified not just how Shakespeare wrote but how English should be spoken and written.[81]

In the previous century, John Milton had also been impressed by Shakespeare's memorable lines, as is evident in his first published poem, "An Epitaph on the admirable Dramaticke Poet, W. SHAKESPEARE."[82] Milton refers to Shakespeare's writing as "Delphick lines": "each heart / Hath from the leaves of thy unvalu'd Booke / Those Delphick lines with deepe Impression tooke."[83] The Oxford Milton takes "Delphick" to mean "inspired, as if coming from the oracle of Apollo, god of poetry, at

Delphi."[84] But the temple at Delphi was also known for its inscriptions: 147 maxims were said to be incised there; the most famous, "know thyself," was incised on a column in the forecourt of the temple.[85] In his *Institutio Oratoria*, Quintilian urges students to copy such maxims on the retentive surfaces of their supple minds.[86] For those ancient oracular inscriptions, young impressionable Milton substitutes lines from Shakespeare's invaluable or "unvalu'd Book." That book is the very book in which the elegy first appeared, the 1632 folio of *Mr. William Shakespeares Comedies, Histories, & Tragedies*, a copy of which we now know Milton owned and marked, including with some 600 scorings of noteworthy passages.[87]

But that is not the only book by Shakespeare that impressed Milton in his formative years. If "unvalu'd" is taken to mean *undervalued* as well as *invaluable*, then the unassuming quarto of the 1609 *Shake-speares Sonnets* may also be intended. As Colin Burrow has observed, Milton's elegy, entitled "An Epitaph" in its 1640 printing, takes as "its point of departure" sonnet 81, the sonnet that figures itself as an epitaph on stone to be read and recited by posterity ("Which eyes not yet created shall o'er-read, / And tongues-to-be your being shall rehearse").[88] Burrow's observation might be extended beyond sonnet 81, for as we saw in Chapter 1, the very conceit of the sonnet as epitaph is exploited in the typography and metaphorics of both the dedication and the sonnets themselves. In sixteen iambic pentameter lines, Milton monumentalizes Shakespeare through the same topos as the Sonnets had the beloved youth. His own "An Epitaph" exemplifies what it describes: the impression Shakespeare makes on his readers. His powers are literally astonishing, reducing readers to stone surfaces bearing the imprint of his texts: "Then thou our fancy of it self bereaving, / Dost make us Marble with too much conceaving." Shakespeare's plays and poems live on in "An Epitaph" not as self-expression but as impressions made on the thoughts and words of those who have taken them in.

***

Since the end of the eighteenth century, the special allure of the Sonnets has been their apparent attachment to Shakespeare. When first incorporated into the canon, it was as writing in Shakespeare's own person, ensconced in a critical apparatus that tethered the poems to both the author's life and to his other works. The text itself, like that of the rest of the canon, aimed to reproduce as closely as possible what Shakespeare was imagined to have written or intended, modified only to emend perceived errors or to modernize spelling and punctuation.

The manuscript tradition and Benson's *Poems*, however, attest to another mode of survival that does just the opposite: that detaches the Sonnets from their authorial source and encourages their movement away from it. Above all, while generally circulating under the auspices of Shakespeare's name, they bear no personal trappings: first- and second-person pronouns remain indefinite, occasions generic, time and place unmarked. Lacking the specificity of reference that would limit their application to the author, they invite appropriation, and without accountability to what is now the inviolable integrity of the text.

Might the future imagined by the 1609 *Sonnets* itself have been in manuscript rather than type? The collection invokes print technology only once and then to reference biological rather than poetic reproduction. In the couplet of sonnet 11, the act by which the youth is to "breed another thee" (sonnet 6) is likened to the signet seal's imprinting of wax: "[Nature] carved thee for her seal, and meant thereby / Thou shouldst print more, not let that copy die." And why stop at one imprint? Why not copy perfection ten times over, "ten for one" (sonnet 6)?

When the poet introduces poetry as an alternative mode of survival to the begetting of children, the metaphor switches from mechanical to horticultural: "I engraft you new" (sonnet 15). The issue will be the result not of breeding but of inscription, as suggested by this verb's Greek root, *graphein*, to carve or to write. The verses consistently refer to themselves as if existing in script rather than print, the work of the pen rather than the press. In sonnet 81, it is the pen that keeps beauty's rose perennial: "You still shall live (such virtue hath my pen)." It may be that the miraculous "might" sonnet 65 ascribes to "black ink" is not of type, then, but of the pen. When the poet refers deictically to "this line," would he not have his own handwritten page before him? And would it not have been the same manuscript page from which the lover reads the poet's self-defeating caveat: "remember not / The hand that writ it" (sonnet 71)? Perhaps it is as copied by other hands that the Sonnets themselves imagine enduring. Might the perpetuity they envisage be through the agency not of mechanical reproduction of the selfsame but of the manuscript proliferation of variant copy? If so, then Benson would have done the Sonnets a good turn by preparing them for an afterlife of handwritten diffusion.

***

Tradition once held that Shakespeare gave no thought to posterity.[89] According to Pope, he wrote plays "[f]or gain, not glory ... / And grew Immortal in his own despight."[90] Had he been concerned for the future, it was assumed, he would have overseen the collecting, preparing, and publishing of his plays. In the preface to his 1765 edition of Shakespeare, Samuel Johnson rejects outright the implication of the Folio compilers that, had Shakespeare lived longer, he would have made provision for his plays. On the contrary, Johnson demurs, Shakespeare had ample time in retirement to prepare his works for posterity, "while he was yet little *declined into the vale of years*."[91] Rather, he set his sights on the immediate present: "It does not appear that Shakespeare thought his works worthy of posterity, that he levied any ideal tribute upon future times, or had any further prospect, than of present popularity and present profit." Johnson, it seems, had not read the 1609 *Sonnets*, at least not at the time he wrote this preface.[92]

Posterity looms large in the Sonnets from their onset. The first two lines of the first sonnet make concern for future generations axiomatic: "From fairest creatures we desire increase, / That thereby beauty's rose might never die." This injunction, unlike the biblical one to "be fruitful and multiply," is strictly exclusive. It calls for the increase only of "fairest creatures." There appears to be only one such creature per generation, as there is only one firstborn to inherit an estate. Yet more than dynasty is at stake in these poems: at risk is the twofold ideal of beauty and truth, symbolized by the show and fragrance of the rose. The rather quaint term the first seventeen sonnets have acquired, "the procreation sonnets," is misleading. For these poems are concerned more with preservation than creation, with sustaining life rather than bringing it into being.[93] The twofold ideal is to be transmitted to posterity like a legacy, through either biological reproduction or poetic imitation. If the present "fairest creature" does not provide for the future by begetting a likeness of himself

("Make thee another self" [sonnet 10]), the world will suffer fatally, as is prognosticated by the couplet of sonnet 14: "Thy end is truth's and beauty's doom and date." It falls on the poet to prevent that fatality, to assure the fairest creature's survival, if not in flesh and blood then through poetry.

Yet beauty's paragon may have been flawed from the start. The youth's "unprovident" (sonnet 10) refusal to make provision for the future signals a deep imperfection and the first group of sonnets finds more to blame than to praise in the idealized creature, charging him with all manner of sin and crime: self-love, gluttony, avarice, onanism, profligacy, parsimony, cruelty, even murder—not only of himself, by suicidally cutting off his lineage, but also of humankind, by the genocidal desire "to stop posterity"(sonnet 3). His self-loving abstinence makes for a ruinous, even holocaustal, precedent: "If all were minded so the times should cease, / And threescore year would make the world away" (sonnet 11).

As if to counter the fairest creature's reckless indifference, the poet takes on the responsibility of providently looking ahead, envisioning the "age to come" (sonnet 17), "times in hope" (sonnet 60), "ages yet to be" (sonnet 101). To 'the "age unbred," (sonnet 104), he attributes embryonic human features and faculties: "eyes not yet created" will read his lines and "tongues-to-be" will give voice to them (sonnet 81) and to their appraisal of their hyperbole, "This poet lies" (sonnet 17). Most alarmingly, in an apostrophe, posterity possesses ears with which to receive the awful news, shouted loud and clear as if across the ages: "[H]ear this thou age unbred: / Ere you were born was beauty's summer dead" (sonnet 104). At some indeterminate future point, perhaps at whatever time the sonnet is being read, the dread outcome of the youth's self-absorption will have already come to pass: a future devoid of "fairest creatures." The proleptic "age unbred" will have arrived: a brood that will be ill-bred, like the creatures sonnet 11 would have had "barrenly perish"—"harsh, featureless, and rude."

In the future he foresees, the poet is himself conspicuously absent, or if present, only in the impossibly posthumous state of his strange self-referencing epithet, "thy deceasèd lover" (32) and "deceasèd I" (72).

Already on his "death-bed" (73), he envisions a time when he is dead ("when I am dead" [71]), interred ("When that churl Death my bones with dust shall cover" [32]), and decomposed ("when I in earth am rotten" [81]). At his own insistence, nothing will remain of him, not even a grave marker—"My name be buried where my body is" (72)—his identity lost among charnel house remains: "The earth can yield me but a common grave" (81). He watches his paragon pace forth through an apocalyptic landscape, before the "eyes of all posterity" (55), though not his own, unless peering from the grave.

In the Sonnets, the promised eternity that caught Thorpe's attention is never extended to the poet. Always it is the verse (or its subject) that is to be kept alive:

> My love shall in my verse ever live young (19)
> Your praise shall still find room, / Even in the eyes of all posterity (55)
> His beauty shall in these black lines be seen, / And they shall live (63)
> You still shall live (such virtue hath my pen) (81)
> Your name from hence immortal life shall have (81)
> Your monument shall be my gentle verse (81)
> And thou in this shalt find thy monument (107)

In the only sonnet in which the poet confers perpetual life on himself, it is not in a durable verse monument but in poetry's smallest and least esteemed particle, an ephemeral coincidence of sound: "I'll live in this poor rhyme" (sonnet 107).

The poet's absence from the future for which he writes does not derive from the immortalizing topos of Shakespeare's ancient models.[94] It is not to be found in Horace, who imagines himself eternalized by his verse: "I shall continually be renewed in the praises of posterity."[95] Nor is it in Ovid, who presumes that his art will prolong his life indefinitely: "My lyfe shall euerlastingly be lengthened still by fame."[96] But it does correspond with the preliminaries to the first comprehensive collection of Shakespeare's plays, the 1623 *Mr. William Shakespeares Comedies, Histories, & Tragedies* and its three seventeenth-century reprints, as well as with its poetic counterpart, the 1640 *Poems: Written by Wil. Shake-speare. Gent.* in its many editions. At the entrance to both collections, Shakespeare's death is lamented, while his works are poised for survival. Thorpe, at the threshold of the 1609 *Sonnets,* performs a similar parting of ways, even in Shakespeare's lifetime, perhaps taking his cue from the Sonnets themselves, where the poet absents himself from the future he imagines for his poems. In all three publications, the works are imagined surviving without the individuating particulars of their author's life. And so indeed they did survive for almost two centuries after Shakespeare's death.

***

This book has been about Shakespeare's long survival without the biography that is now deemed indispensable to the appreciation and understanding of his works. At a certain point, around 1800, that absence is perceived as an inexplicable lack. Why had not those who had lived closer to Shakespeare's time written a biography or at least set aside the personal papers for one? The same incredulity arises in relation to the 1609 *Sonnets*: why had their autobiographical content not been discovered earlier? August Wilhelm Schlegel, in a lecture delivered in Vienna in 1808 and published in London in 1815, disparaged earlier commentators for failing to do so.

> It betrays more than ordinary deficiency of critical acumen in Shakspeare's commentators, that none of them, so far as we know, have ever thought of availing themselves of his sonnets for tracing the circumstances of his life. These sonnets paint most unequivocally the actual situation and sentiments of the poet; they make us acquainted with the passions of the man; they even contain remarkable confessions of his youthful errors.[97]

Yet it is not critical acumen that is lacking but the desire to know Shakespeare first hand, intimately, whether through his handwriting, his personal papers, or in the case of the Sonnets, in writing that could be construed to be personal, private, even confessional. Only when approached with that desire, do the Sonnets appear self-evidently about him.

When Malone takes Shakespeare's punning on "will" in sonnet 136 as self-referential, he is missing an ingenious joke.[98] Does "my name is Will" single out Shakespeare if "William" is the most popular first name in England? (By one estimate, "almost a quarter of the male population were christened William."[99]) More common still is the homonymic diminutive form of William: "will" in signifying both sexual desire and its organ would have applied to the entire male population, perhaps the female one as well.[100] This proper name, instead of differentiating one person from the next, renders persons indistinguishable. It is Will's anonymity that allows him to "pass untold" among his mistress's multiple other lovers, all of whom answer to the same name. The mistress cannot tell them apart from one another, or perhaps even from her own desire.

The identification of the first person with Shakespeare's surname on the title page may look more promising. But the Sonnets hardly invite biographical readings. Persons are unnamed and personal pronouns remain indefinite; in many of them, 'you' and 'thou' remain ungendered.[101] Coordinates of time and place are consistently withheld. Perhaps more unsettling still is the heavy use of deictics whose referents depend on knowing precisely what the sonnets keep to themselves: who is speaking, where and when. They can remain frustratingly indefinite, disorienting the reader with their intense ambiguity: "And that is this, and this with thee remains" (sonnet 74).

The Sonnets' reticence has been differently explained. It has sometimes been speculated that Shakespeare wrote them for himself alone, to work out in verse his own private thoughts and feelings. Or perhaps they were written, as Francis Meres had specified, for a circle of "private friends," who would have been familiar with their particulars.[102] It has also been proposed that details were encrypted in the letters and spaces of the book, to be decoded by their addressee alone. Or was their suppression intended to silence truths that would have been embarrassing or even incriminating if explicit? But the 1640 *Poems* took their opacity another way, as conveniently non-committal and therefore impersonal or transpersonal and suitable for the generically pitched miscellany. Like the anecdote, genre, and compendia of the previous three chapters, the miscellany sends Shakespeare's Sonnets out into a larger discursive orbit rather than limiting them to the self-expression of their titular source.

From 1800 on, Shakespeareans have been straining to extrapolate the particulars of Shakespeare's life from both contemporary documents and, on the model of the Sonnets, from the works themselves. But these particulars were once not only not necessary or desirable but perhaps to be avoided. At least that is what is suggested by what I have described as the epitaphic thresholds of the 1623 Folio as well as of the 1640 miscellany and the 1609 *Sonnets*. Shakespeare's decease rather than his life stands at their forefront. At the moment of publication, the works take leave of their authorial source, no biographical strings attached. The fact of Shakespeare's death in 1616 is paramount, lamented by the elegiac preliminaries as they simultaneously anticipate the posthumous survival of his works. Shakespeare is consigned to the bygone past ("done are *Shakespeares* dayes: / His dayes are done") while his works remain alive to the future.

Notes

Introduction

1 Samuel Schoenbaum, *Shakespeare's Lives*, new edn. (Oxford: Oxford University Press, 1991), vii, 178, 169.

2 Edmond Malone, *The Life of William Shakspeare*, in *The Plays and Poems of William Shakspeare*, ed. Edmond Malone and James Boswell, 21 vols. (London: F. C. and J. Rivington [etc.], 1821), II, 1–525.

3 *The Plays and Poems of William Shakspeare*, ed. Edmond Malone, 10 vols. (1790), I, pt. 1, 102–54.

4 For Malone's specification that the biography be the first volume of his second edition (1821), see the 1796 prospectus appended to *An Inquiry into the Authenticity of Certain Miscellaneous Papers and Legal Instruments* (1796), n.p.

Chapter 1

1 Nicholas Rowe, *Some Account of the Life, & c. of Mr. William Shakespear*, in *The Works of Mr. William Shakespear*, ed. Nicholas Rowe, 6 vols. (1709), I, i–xl.

2 On the transcription of epitaphs by the Society of Antiquaries and their incorporation in verse forms, see Scott Newstok, *Quoting Death in Early Modern England: The Poetics of Epitaphs Beyond the Tomb* (Basingstoke: Palgrave Macmillan, 2009), 4.

3 Edmund Spenser's birthdate appears on his tomb in Westminster Abbey—"He was borne in London in the year 1553 and died in the year 1598"—but it was incised in 1778 when the monument was restored.

4 Anthony Wood, *Athenæ Oxonienses. An Exact History of All the Writers and Bishops Who Have Had Their Education in the Most Ancient and Famous University of Oxford, from ... 1500 to the End of ... 1690 ...* 4 vols. (1691), 1, Titlepage.

5 Adam Smyth, *Autobiography in Early Modern England* (Cambridge: Cambridge University Press, 2010), 6, 159–61.

6 Facsimiles of his baptism and burial entries in the Stratford parish register are accessible through the Folger Shakespeare Library website: https://shakespearedocumented.folger.edu/resource/document/parish-register-entry-recording-william-shakespeares-baptism and https://shakespearedocumented.fol

ger.edu/resource/document/parish-register-entry-recording-william-shake speares-burial.

7 Adam G. Hooks notes that the first notice in print of Shakespeare's death appears in a pamphlet by John Taylor the Water Poet published in 1620. See *Selling Shakespeare: Biography, Bibliography, and the Book Trade* (Cambridge: Cambridge University Press, 2016), 18.

8 While interest in Shakespeare's place of burial is evident throughout the seventeenth century, the first record of his place of birth is dated 1757. See Lena Cowen Orlin, *The Private Life of William Shakespeare* (Oxford: Oxford University Press, 2021), 40.

9 The predecessor of the *DNB*, *Biographia Britannica*, published throughout the second half of the eighteenth century, invariably gives deathdates but rarely birthdates. On the use of deathdates in ordering the lives of artists from Vasari into the eighteenth century, see Ian Verstegen, "Death Dates, Birth Dates, and the Beginnings of Modern Art History," *Storiografia: Rivista annuale di storia*, 10 (2006), 1–19.

10 For Aubrey's "genitures," see Kate Bennett, "General Introduction," in *John Aubrey: Brief Lives with An Apparatus for the Lives of Our English Mathematical Writers*, ed. Kate Bennett, 2 vols. (Oxford: Oxford University Press, 2015), I, cxv–cxvi.

11 Thomas Fuller, *The History of the Worthies of England*, ed. P. Austin Nuttall, 3 vols. (New York: AMS Press, 1965), III, 267–300; for the entry on Shakespeare, see 284–5.

12 William Winstanley, *The Lives of the Most Famous English Poets* (1687), 133.

13 Gerard Langbaine, *An Account of the English Dramatick Poets* (1691), 468.

14 Oldys's copy of Langbaine with "Copious MS. notes" is held by the British Library (C.28.g.1, 469).

15 Malone's heavily annotated interleaved copy of Langbaine is held by the Bodleian Library (MSS. Malone 129–32).

16 Rowe, *Some Account of the Life*, in *The Works of Mr. William Shakespear* (1709), I, xxxiv, ii. On the fixing of the still uncertain birthdate, see Orlin, *The Private Life of William Shakespeare*, 1–3.

17 Malone, *The Life of William Shakspeare*, in *The Plays and Poems of William Shakspeare*, ed. Edmond Malone and James Boswell, 21 vols. (London: F. C. and J. Rivington [etc.], 1821), II, 63, 610 n. 6. This edition will hereafter be referred to as Malone–Boswell 1821.

18 Malone's biography was not reproduced until 1966 when the complete Malone-Boswell 1821 edition was published in facsimile reprint by AMS Press (New York, 1966).

19 I have based my account of Lee's biography on Samuel Schoenbaum, *Shakespeare's Lives*, new edn. (Oxford: Oxford University Press, 1991), 374–82.

20 On Shakespeare's decease as the unifying postulate of the First Folio's preliminaries, see Margreta de Grazia, "Shakespeare's Timeline," *Shakespeare Quarterly*, 65 (2014), 397–8.

21 See Chris Laoutaris, "The Prefatory Material," in Emma Smith, ed., *The Cambridge Companion to Shakespeare's First Folio* (Cambridge: Cambridge University Press, 2016), 48–67, 52.

22 "To the Reader," frontispiece to *Mr. William Shakespeares Comedies, Histories, & Tragedies*, ed. John Heminges and Henry Condell (1623).

23 "To the Great Variety of Readers," in *Mr. William Shakespeares Comedies, Histories, & Tragedies* (1623), A3r.

24 "The Epistle Dedicatorie," in *Mr. William Shakespeares Comedies, Histories, & Tragedies* (1623), A2r–A3v.

25 On the Folio as "a memorial volume" whose preliminaries draw on Horace, Ovid, and the Sonnets, see John Kerrigan, "Shakespeare, Elegy, and Epitaph 1557–1640," in Jonathan Post, ed., *The Oxford Handbook of Shakespeare's Poetry* (Oxford: Oxford University Press, 2013), 241. On the interchangeability of epitaphs, epigrams, and sonnets, see Newstok, *Quoting Death*, 25.

26 Hugh Holland, "Upon the Lines and Life of the Famous Scenicke Poet, Master William Shakespeare," in *Mr. William Shakespeares Comedies, Histories, & Tragedies* (1623), n.p.

27 *Mr. William Shakespeares Comedies, Histories, and Tragedies* (1632), n.p.

28 The copy is held by the Folger Shakespeare Library and is accessible online at https://doi.org/10.37078/203.

29 On the 1640 octavo's miniature mirroring of the 1623 Folio, see Margreta de Grazia, *Shakespeare Verbatim: The Reproduction of Authenticity and the 1790 Apparatus* (Oxford: Oxford University Press, 1991), 166–72.

30 "To the Reader," in *Poems: Written by Wil. Shake-speare. Gent.*, ed. John Benson (1640), n.p.

31 In addition to the five versions in print, thirty-five manuscript copies of Basse's epitaph have been discovered. See Alan H. Nelson, "Manuscript Copy of William Basse's Elegy on William Shakespeare," *Shakespeare Documented*, last modified January 25, 2020, https://doi.org/10.37078/573.

32 The preface to the first edition of *Othello* (1622) also identifies itself as posthumous, "the Author being dead." See Hooks, *Selling Shakespeare*, 23.

33 *The Oxford Shakespeare: The Complete Sonnets and Poems*, ed. Colin Burrow (Oxford: Oxford University Press, 2002), 491.

34 Schoenbaum, *Shakespeare's Lives*, 87.

35 Rowe, *Some Account of the Life*, in *The Works of Mr. William Shakespear* (1709), I, v. Subsequent references to Rowe's Life will appear parenthetically in text by page number.

36 *Lexicons of Early Modern English*, s.v. "extravagance," accessed September 15, 2021, http://leme.library.utoronto.ca.

37 For a full account of this anecdote's genealogy, see T. W. Baldwin, "Run-away Shakspere," in *William Shakspere's Small Latine & Lesse Greeke*, 2 vols. (Urbana: University of Illinois Press, 1944), II, 681–9. For an earlier, more incriminating version of the anecdote than in Rowe, in which Shakespeare is "oft whipped and sometimes imprisoned," see Schoenbaum, *Shakespeare's Lives*, 69.

38 Samuel Johnson, preface to *The Plays of William Shakespeare*, ed. Samuel Johnson, 8 vols. (1765), I, clii.

39 On the crushing expense of procuring French dancers, see David Roberts, *Thomas Betterton: The Greatest Actor of the Restoration Stage* (Cambridge: Cambridge University Press, 2010), 168. On the "prix exorbitant" commanded by Senesino, a celebrated castrato from Sienna for whom Handel wrote arias, see Jonathan Keates, *Handel: The Man and His Music*, rev. edn. (London: Bodley Head, 2008), 167.

40 John Manningham, *Diary*, quoted by Schoenbaum, *Shakespeare's Lives*, 17.

41 As recounted by Aubrey in his Life of Sir William Davenant. See *Aubrey: Brief Lives*, I, 140.

42 Schoenbaum, *Shakespeare's Lives*, 78.

43 For the "Epitaph on Himself," see *The Oxford Shakespeare: The Complete Works*, ed. Stanley Wells et al., 2nd edn. (Oxford: Oxford University Press, 2005), 783. For the source of the attribution in a letter by the antiquary John Dowdall, dated April 10, 1693, see Schoenbaum, *Shakespeare's Lives*, 83.

44 See Alfred Corn, "Shakespeare's Epitaph," *Hudson Review*, 64 (2011), 295–303.

45 Stephen Greenblatt, "The Traces of Shakespeare's Life," in Margreta de Grazia and Stanley Wells, eds., *The New Cambridge Companion to Shakespeare* (Cambridge: Cambridge University Press, 2010), 4. On Shakespeare's near invisibility in the "disciplinary archive," see also Orlin, *The Private Life of William Shakespeare*, 70.

46 See Stephen Greenblatt, *Shakespeare's Freedom* (Chicago: University of Chicago Press, 2010), 14.

47 Malone–Boswell 1821, II, 472; *The Plays and Poems of William Shakspeare*, ed. Edmond Malone, 10 vols. (1790), I, pt. 1, lxiii.

48 Charles Gildon, "Critical Remarks," in *The Works of Mr. William Shakespear: Volume the Seventh*, ed. Charles Gildon (1710), vii–viii.

49 "To the Great Variety of Readers," in *Mr. William Shakespeares Comedies, Histories, & Tragedies* (1623), A3.

50 Ben Jonson, *Discoveries*, ed. Lorna Hutson, in *The Cambridge Edition of the Works of Ben Jonson*, gen. eds. David Bevington, Martin Butler, and Ian Donaldson, 7 vols. (Cambridge: Cambridge University Press, 2012), VII, 521–2.

51 Alexander Pope, *The First Epistle of the Second Book of Horace, Imitated* (1737), 16.

52 See Sarah van den Berg, "Marking His Place: Ben Jonson's Punctuation," *Early Modern Literary Studies*, 1 (1995), 2.1–25.

53 Johnson, preface to *The Plays of William Shakespeare* (1765), I, clii.

54 Johnson, preface to *The Plays of William Shakespeare* (1765), I, clii.

55 Letter from Malone to the Rev. James Davenport, quoted in James Prior, *Life of Edmond Malone, Editor of Shakespeare*, 2 vols. (London: Smith, Elder & Co., 1860), I, 284.

56 Johnson, preface to *The Plays of William Shakespeare* (1765), I, xxxvi.

57 Humphrey Moseley, "The Stationer to the Reader," in *The Comedies and Tragedies Written by Francis Beaumont and Iohn Fletcher* (1647), A4v. Scholars have questioned John Fletcher's matriculation, but as Arata Ide points out, "Certainly Fletcher's contemporaries widely regarded him as a university-trained playwright." See "John Fletcher of Corpus Christi College: New Records of His Early Years," *Early Theatre*, 13 (2010), 63.

58 Thomas Nashe, "To the Gentlemen Students of Both Universities," preface to *Menaphon: Camillas Alarum to Slumbering Euphues*, by Robert Greene (1589), n.p.

59 Henry Chettle and Robert Greene, *Greene's Groatsworth of Wit*, ed. D. Allen Carroll (New York: Medieval & Renaissance Texts & Studies, 1994), 84–5. For the debate over the pamphlet's authorship, see Carroll's introduction, 1–31.

60 For a similar standoff between scholarly university playwrights and popular players who, like Shakespeare, turn playwright, see *The Second Part of the Return from Parnassus* in the anonymous *The Three Parnassus Plays*, ed. J. B Leishman (London: Ivor Nicholson & Watson, 1949). See esp. the editor's introduction, 58–60, and 4.3.1753–76.

61 For the plagiarism theory and its refutation, see Brian Vickers, "'Upstart Crow'? The Myth of Shakespeare's Plagiarism," *The Review of English Studies*, 68 (April 2017), 244–67.

62 *King Henry VI, Part Three*, ed. John D. Cox and Eric Rasmussen, Arden Shakespeare, 3rd ser. (London: Bloomsbury, 2001), 1.4.137.

63 Euripides, *Medea*, in *Cyclops. Alcestis. Medea*, ed. and trans. David Kovacs (Cambridge, MA: Harvard University Press, 1994), line 1345; Seneca, *Medea*, in *Hercules. Trojan Women. Phoenician Women. Medea. Phaedra*, ed. and trans. John G. Fitch (Cambridge, MA: Harvard University Press, 2002), line 863.

64 *The Seventh Tragedie of Seneca, Entitled Medea*, trans. John Studley (1566), 41v. For Shakespeare's use of Studley, see Katherine Heavey, "'An infant of the house of York': Medea and Absyrtus in Shakespeare's First Tetralogy," *Comparative Drama*, 50 (2016), 235–7.

65 "To Mr: Ben: Jonson," quoted in Mark Bland, "Francis Beaumont's Verse Letters to Ben Jonson and 'The Mermaid Club,'" in Peter Beal and A. S. G. Edwards, eds., *Scribes and Transmission in English Manuscripts 1400–1700*, English Manuscript Studies 1100–1700 12 (London: British Library, 2005), 175.

66 Schoenbaum, *Shakespeare's Lives*, 85.

67 Fuller, *The History of the Worthies of England*, 245.

68 Edward Phillips, *Theatrum Poetarum, or, A Compleat Collection of the Poets* (1675), 194.

69 *Aubrey: Brief Lives*, I, 366.

70 *Titus Andronicus*, ed. Jonathan Bate, rev. edn., Arden Shakespeare, 3rd ser. (London: Bloomsbury, 2018), 4.2.22–3 and n. 23.

71 From Sir Nicholas L'Estrange, *Merry Passages and Jests*, quoted by Schoenbaum, *Shakespeare's Lives*, 56.

72 For the origin of this rumor in Fuller's *Worthies* and the absence of substantiating records at either the college or university, see Ian Donaldson, "Life of Ben Jonson," in *The Cambridge Edition of the Works of Ben Jonson Online* (Cambridge: Cambridge University Press, 2014), https://universitypublishingonline. org/cambridge/benjonson/k/essays/jonsons_life_essay/.

73 From a note in Aubrey's unpublished *Chronologia Vestiaria*, as quoted by Kate Bennett in "Shakespeare's Monument at Stratford: A New Seventeenth-Century Account," *Notes and Queries*, 47 (2000), 464.

74 Nikolaus Pevsner and Alexandra Wedgwood, *Warwickshire: The Buildings of England* (London: Penguin Books, 1966), 413. For Pevsner's identification of funereal statuary with scholars and divines, see Orlin, *The Private Life of William Shakespeare*, 403–4 n. 55.

75 Orlin, *The Private Life of William Shakespeare*, 244, 282–3, 252.

76 For Tonson's project of canon-making by complementing his publication of Greek and Latin translations with modern vernacular works, see Peter Holland, introduction to *The Works of Mr. William Shakespear, edited by Nicholas Rowe, 1709*, 7 vols. (London: Pickering and Chatto, 1999), I, viii; and Robert B. Hamm, Jr., "Rowe's Shakespeare (1709) and the Tonson House Style," *College Literature*, 31 (2004), 179–205.

77 Francis Meres, *Palladis Tamia. Wits Treasury, Being the Second Part of Wits Common Wealth* (1598), 279r–287r.

78 Johnson, preface to *The Plays of William Shakespeare* (1765), I, xlvii.

79 See T. S. R. Boase, "Illustrations of Shakespeare's Plays in the Seventeenth and Eighteenth Centuries," *Journal of the Warburg and Courtauld Institutes*, 10 (1947), 86.

80 Gildon, "An Essay on the Art, Rise and Progress of the Stage," in *The Works of Mr. William Shakespear: Volume the Seventh*, viii.

81 Thomas Warton, *The History of English Poetry, from the Close of the Eleventh to the Commencement of the Eighteenth Century*, 3 vols. (1781), III, 499.

82 Hugh Blair, *Lectures on Rhetoric and Belles Lettres*, 2 vols. (1783), II, 523.

83 Gildon, "An Essay on the Art, Rise and Progress of the Stage," ii–iii, xi, vii, xxii. For debates on Shakespeare's knowledge of the ancients, see Paul D. Cannan, "Early Shakespeare Criticism, Charles Gildon, and the Making of Shakespeare the Playwright-Poet," *Modern Philology*, 102 (August 2004), 35–55.

84 Alexander Pope, preface to *The Works of Shakespear*, ed. Alexander Pope, 6 vols. (1725), I, iv, xxxvii.

85 Johnson, preface to *The Plays of William Shakespeare* (1765), I, xvii.

86 John Dryden, preface to *Troilus and Cressida, or, Truth Found Too Late ... to which is Prefix'd, a Preface Containing the Grounds of Criticism in Tragedy* (1679).

87 Nahum Tate, "Epistle Dedicatory," in *The History of King Lear: Acted at the Duke's Theatre* (1681), n.p.

88 Samuel Taylor Coleridge, *The Literary Remains of Samuel Taylor Coleridge*, ed. Henry Nelson Coleridge, 2 vols. (London: William Pickering, 1836–39), II, 61.

89 Samuel Taylor Coleridge, *Notes and Lectures upon Shakespeare and Some of the Old Poets and Dramatists*, ed. Mrs. H.N. Coleridge (London: William Pickering, 1849), I, 61. Coleridge elsewhere credits another critic: "It was Lessing who first proved to all thinking men, even to Shakespeare's own countrymen, the true nature of his apparent irregularities." See *Biographia Literaria; or, Biographical Sketches of My Literary Life and Opinions*, 2 vols. (London: Rest Fenner, 1817), I, xxiii.

90 See Coleridge, *Biographia Literaria*, I, 257.

91 William Wordsworth, "Essay, Supplementary to the Preface," in *Poems by William Wordsworth: Including Lyrical Ballads, and the Miscellaneous Pieces of the Author*, 2 vols. (London: Longman, Hurst, Rees, Orme, and Brown, 1815), I, 352.

92 Charles Knight, *Passages of a Writing Life during Half a Century: with a Prelude of Early Reminiscences* (London: Knight & Co., 1873), 287.

Chapter 2

1 On the necessarily conjectural status of the date of a play's composition— as opposed to of its registration, performance, or publication—see Margreta de Grazia, *Four Shakespearean Period Pieces* (Chicago: University of Chicago Press, 2021), 60–105.

2 Joseph Priestley, *A Description of a Chart of Biography*, 4th edn. (1770), 5.

3 Horace, *Odes* in *Odes and Epodes*, ed. and trans. Niall Rudd (Cambridge, MA: Harvard University Press, 2004), 3.29.33–4.

4 Priestley, *A Description of a Chart of Biography*, 23–24.

5 Daniel Rosenberg and Anthony Grafton, *Cartographies of Time: A History of the Timeline* (New York: Princeton Architectural Press, 2010), 19.

6 Priestley, *A Description of a Chart of Biography*, 14, 6.

7 Although his *Life of William Shakspeare* was published as volume 2 of his posthumous 1821 edition, Malone had intended it to be volume 1, as he specifies in the prospectus for his second edition, appended to *An Inquiry into the Authenticity of Certain Miscellaneous Papers and Legal Instruments* (1796), n.p.

8 James Boswell, Jr. "A Biographical Memoir of the Late Edmond Malone," in *The Plays and Poems of William Shakspeare*, ed. Edmond Malone and James Boswell, 21 vols. (London: F. C. and J. Rivington [etc.], 1821) I, lv. On Malone's role as "midwife" to Boswell's biography of Johnson, see Peter Martin, *Edmond Malone, Shakespearean Scholar* (Cambridge: Cambridge University Press, 1995), 144.

9 *The Private Papers of Boswell from Malahide Castle 1785–89*, quoted by Martin, *Edmond Malone*, 150.

10 James Boswell, Sr., "Advertisement," in *The Life of Samuel Johnson ... Comprehending an Account of His Studies and Numerous Works in Chronological Order*, 2 vols. (1791), I, 4.

11 Boswell, Sr. "Advertisement," in *The Life of Samuel Johnson*, I, 10.

12 On Johnson's attempt to dissuade Malone from rearranging Pope's works and correspondence "in order of time," see Martin, *Edmond Malone*, 57. On Malone's work toward an edition of Aubrey's *Brief Lives*, see Chapter 3.

13 *Poems and Plays by Oliver Goldsmith ... to which is Prefixed the Life of the Author* (1780), i–ix.

14 Malone, "Some Account of the Life and Writings of John Dryden," in *The Critical and Miscellaneous Prose Works of John Dryden*, 4 vols. (London: T. Cadell, Jr. & W. Davies, 1800), I, pt. 1, 2.

15 Malone, "Some Account of the Life and Writings of John Dryden," I, pt. 1, 218–29. For Dryden's "Catalogue ... putting the plays in the Order I wrote them," see the advertisement to his *King Arthur: or, The British Worthy. A Dramatick Opera* (1691).

16 Malone, "Some Account of the Life and Writings of Sir Joshua Reynolds," in *The Works of Sir Joshua Reynolds*, 3 vols. (London: T. Cadell, Jr. & W. Davies, 1801), I, lxxv.

17 The essay, *An Attempt to Ascertain the Order in which the Plays Attributed to Shakspeare Were Written*, included the seven "dubious" plays appended to the 1664/5 Folio and was published in *The Plays of William Shakespeare*, ed. Samuel Johnson and George Steevens (1778), I, 269–346. It was republished without the appended plays and retitled *An Attempt to Ascertain the Order in which the Plays of Shakspeare Were Written* in the Johnson–Steevens–Reed edition of 1785 (I, 283–357). A revised version was published in Malone's 1790 edition (I, 261–386) and was revised again for his second edition (Malone–Boswell 1821, II, 288–468). For a critical appreciation of Malone's chronological determinations

and his revisions of them, see Tiffany Stern, *Shakespeare, Malone and the Problems of Chronology* (Cambridge: Cambridge University Press, 2023. I am grateful to the author for the chance to read this book in draft.

18 Edward Capell, *Notes and Various Readings*, 3 vols. (1779–83), II, 83–6.

19 Malone, "Prospectus," appended to *An Inquiry into the Authenticity*, n.p.

20 Malone–Boswell 1821, II, 238 n. 1. Unless otherwise noted, all quotations from Malone's editions of Shakespeare will be from Malone–Boswell 1821 and will be cited parenthetically in the text by volume and page number.

21 In completing Malone's 1821 essay, Boswell references two rival chronologies, by Alexander Chalmers and Nathan Drake. See Malone-Boswell 1821, II. 470–1. For Hurdis and Coleridge, see de Grazia, *Four Shakespearean Period Pieces*, 86–93.

22 *The Plays and Poems of William Shakspeare*, ed. Edmond Malone, 10 vols. (1790), I, pt. 1, lxiii.

23 As Richard Schoch has demonstrated, Malone also invalidated traditional accounts of stage history in the process of writing his own document-driven history. See *Writing the History of the British Stage, 1660–1900* (Cambridge: Cambridge University Press, 2016), 262–5, 278–81.

24 Letter from the Earl of Charlemont, August 18, 1777, quoted in James Prior, *Life of Edmond Malone, Editor of Shakespeare* (London: Smith, Elder & Co., 1860), 51–2.

25 Nicholas Rowe, *Some Account of the Life, &c. of Mr. William Shakespear*, in *The Works of Mr. William Shakespear*, ed. Nicholas Rowe, 6 vols. (1709), I, ix–x.

26 Letter to the Rev. James Davenport, vicar of Stratford-on-Avon, April 1793, quoted by Samuel Schoenbaum, *Shakespeare's Lives*, new edn. (Oxford: Oxford University Press, 1991), 169.

27 Schoenbaum, *Shakespeare's Lives*, 178.

28 A facsimile edition of Malone–Boswell 1821 was published in 1966 by AMS Press.

29 Sidney Lee, *A Life of William Shakespeare* (London: Smith, Elder & Co., 1898), xiii–xxiii.

30 Sidney Lee, "General Introduction," in *The Complete Works of William Shakespeare*, ed. Sidney Lee, 20 vols. (New York: Harper Brothers, 1906–8), I, xii.

31 For Malone's endorsement of Richard Farmer's *Essay on Shakespeare's Learning* (1767), see Malone–Boswell 1821, II, 103.

32 Stephen Orgel, "Shakespeare and the Kinds of Drama," *Critical Inquiry*, 6 (Autumn 1979), 107–23.

33 Meres, *Palladis Tamia*, 282v–r.

34 On the Folio's grouping of the ten plays sourced in chronicle history into a discrete generic unit, see Margreta de Grazia, *"Hamlet" without Hamlet*

(Cambridge: Cambridge University Press, 2007), 52–3. On Ben Jonson's tacit rejection of the histories as a genre and on the Folio's attempt to consolidate them as a formal unit, see Adam G. Hooks, "Making Histories; or, Shakespeare's Ring," in Heidi Brayman Hackel, Jesse M. Lander, and Zachary Lesser, eds., *The Book in History, the Book as History: New Intersections of the Material Text* (New Haven, CT: Yale University Press, 2016), 345–51.

35 *The Dramatic Works of Shakespeare*, ed. Alexander Chalmers (London: William Pickering, 1826), Contents, n.p.

36 Samuel Johnson, preface to *The Plays of William Shakespeare*, ed. Samuel Johnson, 8 vols. (1765), I, xv.

37 Rowe, *Some Account of the Life*, in *The Works of Mr. William Shakespear* (1709), I, xvii.

38 Alexander Pope, preface to *The Works of Shakespear*, ed. Alexander Pope, 6 vols. (1725), I.

39 Charles Gildon, "An Essay on the Art, Rise and Progress of the Stage," in *The Works of Mr. William Shakespear: Volume the Seventh*, ed. Charles Gildon (1710), ii–iii.

40 Charles Gildon, "Critical Remarks," in *The Works of Mr. William Shakespear: Volume the Seventh*, 347, 258, 337.

41 Gildon, "An Essay on the Art, Rise and Progress of the Stage," ix.

42 Gildon, "Critical Remarks," 463–4.

43 *The Pictorial Edition of the Works of Shakspere*, ed. Charles Knight, 2nd edn., 7 vols. (London: G. Routledge & Sons, 1867), I, 6.

44 John Payne Collier, *Reasons for a New Edition of Shakespeare's Works* (London: Whittaker & Co., 1841), 48.

45 F. J. Furnivall, "The Founder's Prospectus," in *The New Shakspere Society's Transactions* (London: N. Trübner & Co., 1874), I, 6–7 n. 3.

46 For Nicolaus Delius's German edition (1854–61) and Georg Gottfried Gervinus's critical commentary (1849–50), as well as the translation of both into English, see de Grazia, *Four Shakespearean Period Pieces*, 94.

47 For the fourfold schema, see Edward Dowden, *Shakspere*, Literature Primers (New York: D. Appleton & Co., 1878), 47–57; and in table format, *Shakspere: A Critical Study of His Mind and Art* (London: Henry S. King & Co., 1875), viii–ix. Dowden makes this pronouncement in both his primer (*Shakspere*, 5) and in revised editions of *Shakspere: A Critical Study* (358). On "late writing" as a biographical category that presupposes the concept of chronological development as well as of a self-contained canon, see Gordon McMullan, *Shakespeare and the Idea of Late Writing: Authorship in the Proximity of Death* (Cambridge: Cambridge University Press, 2007), 136–60.

Chapter 3

1 See Samuel Schoenbaum, *Shakespeare's Lives*, new edn. (Oxford: Oxford University Press, 1991), 178.

2 For the documents in print, see Samuel Schoenbaum, *William Shakespeare: Records and Images* (London: Scolar Press, 1981). For the documents online, see the Folger Shakespeare Library website: https://shakespearedocumented. folger.edu. For Malone's role in the prehistory of the digitalization of the Shakespearean archive, see Alan Galey, *The Shakespearean Archive: Experiments in New Media from the Renaissance to Postmodernity* (Cambridge: Cambridge University Press, 2014), 1–5.

3 Not until the early decades of the twentieth century were three pages of the theatrical manuscript "The Booke of Sir Thomas Moore" considered to be in Shakespeare's hand. See John Jowett's Arden edition of *Sir Thomas More* (London: Bloomsbury, 2011), Appendix 5, 461–9.

4 Edmond Malone, *The Life of William Shakspeare*, in *The Plays and Poems of William Shakspeare*, ed. Edmond Malone and James Boswell, 21 vols. (London: F. C. and J. Rivington [etc.], 1821), II, 486. This edition will hereafter be referred to as Malone–Boswell 1821.

5 Malone, *Life of William Shakspeare*, in Malone–Boswell 1821, II, 11. For a passionate defense of his "biographical researches," see II, 26–8 n. 5.

6 Roger Chartier, *The Author's Hand and the Printer's Mind* (Oxford: Polity Press, 2013), 82.

7 Edmond Malone, *An Inquiry into the Authenticity of Certain Miscellaneous Papers and Legal Instruments* (1796), 117.

8 For Malone's account of his acquisition of the Blackfriars Gatehouse title deed, see the preface to his transcript of the "Mortgage Made by Shakspeare A.D. 1612–1613," in Malone–Boswell 1821, II, 591–2.

9 A digital copy of the title deed is available through the Folger Shakespeare Library website: https://shakespearedocumented.folger.edu/resource/ document/shakespeare-purchases-blackfriars-gatehouse-mortgage-signed- shakespeare.

10 Alan H. Nelson and the Folger Shakespeare Library staff identify the initials HL on the seal as those of the scribe's servant, Henry Lawrence: https://shakespearedocumented.folger.edu/resource/document/shakespeare- purchases-blackfriars-gatehouse-mortgage-signed-shakespeare.

11 Malone, *Life of William Shakspeare*, in Malone–Boswell 1821, II, 591.

12 Letter from Malone to his father, April 18, 1767, quoted by Peter Martin, *Edmond Malone, Shakespearean Scholar* (Cambridge: Cambridge University Press, 1995), 11.

13 Malone, "Some Account of the Life and Writings of John Dryden," in *The Critical and Miscellaneous Prose Works of John Dryden*, 4 vols. (London: T. Cadell, Jr. & W. Davies, 1800), I, pt. 1, 2.

14 Malone, *Historical Account of the English Stage*, in Malone–Boswell 1821, III, 361. For an excellent account of how Malone's documents superseded other forms of theatrical record in his history of the stage, see Richard Schoch, *Writing the History of the British Stage, 1660–1900* (Cambridge: Cambridge University Press, 2016), 255–93.

15 These dates are taken from Malone's correspondence with the vicar of Stratford. See Martin, *Edmond Malone*, 129–30.

16 Schoenbaum, *Shakespeare's Lives*, 171–2 Martin, *Edmond Malone*, 179–83.

17 See the commentary on the Blackfriars Gatehouse deed on the Folger Shakespeare Library website: https://shakespearedocumented.folger.edu/resource/document/shakespeare-purchases-blackfriars-gatehouse-mortgage-signed-shakespeare.

18 Malone appears to have cut out autographs from Henslowe's manuscript— for example, of the player John Duke and the poet George Chapman. In *An Inquiry into the Authenticity*, he produces facsimiles of many of them in order to expose the forgeries of William-Henry Ireland (see plate 2, 137v). Kathryn James begins her *English Paleography and Manuscript Culture, 1500–1800* (New Haven, CT: Yale University Press, 2020) with Malone's analysis and exposure of Ireland's forgeries.

19 On the disappearance of both the office-book and Malone's transcript, see Ivan Lupić, "Malone's Double Falsehood," in David Carnegie and Gary Taylor, eds., *The Quest for Cardenio: Shakespeare, Fletcher, Cervantes, and the Lost Play* (Oxford: Oxford University Press, 2012), 95–114. See also E. Collings, "Ghosts in the Archive: Edmond Malone, Craven Ord, and the Missing Texts of Henry Herbert's Office-Book," *The Critical Quarterly*, 55 (2013), 30–41.

20 See Kate Bennett, "General Introduction," in *John Aubrey: Brief Lives with An Apparatus for the Lives of Our English Mathematical Writers*, ed. Kate Bennett, 2 vols. (Oxford: Oxford University Press, 2015), I, cxxxiv–cxxxv.

21 On the bequest of Malone's library to the Bodleian, where it largely remains (as Malone's archive, not Shakespeare's), see Martin, *Edmond Malone*, Appendix A, 277–9.

22 Malone, *Life of William Shakspeare*, in Malone–Boswell 1821, II, 583, 610.

23 From *The Notebooks of Samuel Taylor Coleridge*, quoted by Younglim Han, *Romantic Shakespeare: From Stage to Page* (Cranbury, NJ: Fairleigh Dickinson University Press, 2001), 73.

24 Letter from Joseph Green to James West, September 17, 1747, quoted by Schoenbaum, *Shakespeare's Lives*, 92–3.

25 Malone, *Life of William Shakspeare*, in Malone–Boswell 1821, II, 604 n. 6.

26 Letter believed to be from probably Sir Nathaniel Wraxall to Malone, November 30, 1802, quoted in Schoenbaum, *Shakespeare's Lives*, 171.

27 Malone, *Life of William Shakspeare*, in Malone–Boswell 1821, II, 486.

28 Letter from Malone to Thomas Percy (undated), quoted in Schoenbaum, *Shakespeare's Lives*, 177.

29 Letter from Malone to Boswell, September 1, 1793, quoted in Martin, *Edmond Malone*, 180.

30 Malone, *Life of William Shakspeare*, in Malone–Boswell 1821, II, 486.

31 Malone, *Life of William Shakspeare*, in Malone–Boswell 1821, II, 505–6.

32 I draw here on Schoch's account of Malone's yearning for documents that eluded him; see *Writing the History of the British Stage*, 281–7.

33 Malone, *Historical Account of the English Stage*, in Malone-Boswell 1821, III, 360–1, 180.

34 Letter from Malone to Thomas Warton, August 17, 1789, and from Warton to Malone, August 20, 1789, quoted in Martin, *Edmond Malone*, 126.

35 *Sonnets*, in *Supplement to the Edition of Shakspeare's Plays Published in 1778 by Samuel Johnson and George Steevens*, ed. Edmond Malone, 2 vols. (1780), I, 643 n. 5.

36 For the "bundle of letters and diverse other matters" found in the closet of Shakespeare's associate Richard Quiney, all of them relating to business and legal matters, see Lena Cowen Orlin, *The Private Life of William Shakespeare* (Oxford: Oxford University Press, 2021), Appendix 2, 267–71.

37 Lewis Theobald, preface to *The Works of Shakespeare*, ed. Lewis Theobald, 7 vols. (1733), I, xiv–xv.

38 For an account of the discovery of the "oaken chest," see Ellen MacKay, "Acting Historical with Shakespeare, or, William-Henry Ireland's Oaken Chest," in Peter Holland, ed., *Shakespeare Survey* (Cambridge: Cambridge University Press, 2014), 202–20. For a satirical engraving of the chest's discovery, see James, *English Paleography and Manuscript Culture*, fig. 2, 8–11.

39 Samuel Ireland, *Miscellaneous Papers and Legal Instruments under the Hand and Seal of W. Shakespeare: Including the Tragedy of King Lear, and a Small Fragment of Hamlet, from the Original MSS. in the Possession of Samuel Ireland, of Norfolk Street* (1796).

40 Ireland, preface to *Miscellaneous Papers and Legal Instruments*, 9.

41 John Dryden, prologue to *The Tempest, or The Enchanted Island* (1670), n.p.

42 William-Henry Ireland, *The Confessions of William-Henry Ireland: Containing the Particulars of His Fabrication of the Shakspeare Manuscripts* (London: Ellerton and Byworth, for T. Goddard, 1805), 30–3.

43 Ireland, *Confessions*, 45, 46.

44 Ireland says he copied the signature from the Johnson–Steevens 1778 edition (*Confessions*, 46), but at the time of his fabrication (c. 1795), the mortgage deed had been reproduced only in Malone's 1790 edition (I, pt. 2, 192).

45 On the fabrication and reception of "the Quintin," see Ireland, *Confessions*, 52–5.

46 On Ireland's "Formation of Letters," see *Confessions*, 60.

47 Malone, *An Inquiry into the Authenticity*, 124.

48 Malone, *An Inquiry into the Authenticity*, 121–4.

49 On the inconsistency of autographs, see Malone, *Life of William Shakspeare*, in Malone–Boswell 1821, II, 1–3 n. 1.

50 Malone, *Life of William Shakspeare*, in Malone–Boswell 1821, II, 2 n. 1.

51 Malone, *An Inquiry into the Authenticity*, 121, 120. Malone similarly defends his dropping of the medial *e* in Shakespeare's surname: "He spelt his name himself as I have just now written it, without the middle *e*. Let this therefore for ever decide the question." See *Life of William Shakspeare*, in Malone–Boswell 1821, II, 591.

52 Malone, *An Inquiry into the Authenticity*, 117. Malone publishes a facsimile of Ireland's forgery of Malone's idealized Shakespeare signature (with the fallacious a and r) in *An Inquiry into the Authenticity*, 137v.

53 Malone, "Prospectus," appended to *An Inquiry into the Authenticity*, n.p. Though described in the 1796 prospectus as being "nearly ready for the Press," Malone's "new life" was unfinished at his death in 1812 and was completed by Boswell in 1821.

54 Chartier, *The Author's Hand*, 79.

55 Malone, *Life of William Shakspeare*, in Malone–Boswell 1821, II, 211, n. 2. Subsequent references to this work will be given parenthetically in the text by volume and page number.

56 MSS. Malone 129–32, Bodleian Library, Oxford; MSS. Eng. Misc. d. 26–7, Bodleian Library, Oxford.

57 Malone, "Some Account of the Life and Writings of John Dryden," in *The Critical and Miscellaneous Prose Works of John Dryden*, I, pt. 1, 56.

58 MS. Eng. Misc. d. 26, 70v, Bodleian Library, Oxford.

59 Gerard Langbaine, *An Account of the English Dramatick Poets* (1691). Subsequent references to this work will appear parenthetically in the text by page number.

60 For a sampling of the many authors who extended Langbaine's account into the late seventeenth and eighteenth centuries, see Paulina Kewes, "Shakespeare's Lives in Print, 1662–1821," in Robin Myers, Michael Harris, and Giles Mandelbrote, eds., *Lives in Print: Biography and the Book Trade from the Middle Ages to the 21st Century* (New Castle, DE: Oak Knoll Press, 2002), 59, 79 n. 3.

61   MS. Malone 132, Bodleian Library, Oxford, marginal inscription on p. 469 of his interleaved copy of Langbaine. See also Chapter 1.

62   In annotating their copies of Langbaine, both William Oldys and Thomas Percy criticize Langbaine's chronology. See Schoch, *Writing the History of the English Stage*, 112–13.

63   MS. Malone 129, ff. 31v, 31r.

64   James Caulfield, *An Enquiry into the Conduct of Edmond Malone, Concerning the Manuscript Papers of John Aubrey* (1797), 8.

65   Bennett, "General Introduction," in *Aubrey: Brief Lives*, I, cxliii.

66   Bennett, "General Introduction," in *Aubrey: Brief Lives*, I, lxxvi. On Aubrey's ambivalence toward print publication, see Kate Bennett, "John Aubrey and the Printed Book," *Huntington Library Quarterly*, 76 (2013), 393–411.

67   Nine of Aubrey's Lives were published previously in a sumptuous volume by James Caulfield, *The Oxford Cabinet; Consisting of Engravings from Original Pictures, in the Ashmolean Museum, and Other Public and Private Collections; with Biographical Anecdotes, by John Aubrey, F.R.S.* (1797).

68   Bennett, "General Introduction," in *Aubrey: Brief Lives*, I, lxxix.

69   On the archival imperative "that records be preserved in the order given to them by the entity that created them," see Galey, *The Shakespearean Archive*, 68.

70   Bennett, "General Introduction."

71   MS Aubrey 7, f.1.

72   On Aubrey's intention to place Sir Petty's Life first, see Bennett, "General Introduction," in *Aubrey: Brief Lives*, I, cx, cxiv.

73   John Aubrey, *"Brief Lives," Chiefly of Contemporaries, Set Down by John Aubrey, between the Years 1669 and 1696*, ed. Andrew Clark, 2 vols. (Oxford: Clarendon Press, 1898), II, 225.

74   Bennett, "General Introduction," in *Aubrey: Brief Lives*, I, cxiii–cxiv.

75   *Aubrey: Brief Lives*, I, 162.

76   MS. Eng. Misc. d. 27, f. 236v.

77   MS. Eng. Misc. d. 26, ff. 24v, 24r, 26v.

78   MS. Malone 33, f. 73; MS. Eng. Misc. d. 26, f. 34v.

79   See Bennett, "General Introduction," in *Aubrey: Brief Lives*, I, ciii. For Aubrey's collecting of nativities, see I, cxv–cxvi.

80   *Aubrey: Brief Lives*, I, 39.

81   See Bennett, "General Introduction," in *Aubrey: Brief Lives*, I, xciv.

82   See Bennett, "General Introduction," in Aubrey: *Brief Lives*, I, xci.

83   *Aubrey: Brief Lives*, I, 116.

84   MS. Eng. Misc. d. 26, f. 94v.

85   *Aubrey: Brief Lives*, I, 22; MS. Eng. Misc. d. 27, f. 238v.

86 MS. Eng. Misc. d. 26, ff. 34r, 236v. For a more sympathetic account of Aubrey's character, see Malone's "Character of Aubrey, Antiquarian," in Malone–Boswell 1821, II, 694–7.

87 On the technical sense of "direction" in the casting of horoscopes, see *Aubrey: Brief Lives*, II, 1358, note to lines 9–10.

88 I have pieced together this account from "The Life of John Aubrey," in *Aubrey: Brief Lives*, I, 429–38. For a more detailed chronicle of the astrologically driven incidents of his life, see his chronologically ordered astrological notes, "Accidents of John Aubrey," I, 439–42.

89 See Bennett, "General Introduction," in *Aubrey: Brief Lives*, I, lxxvii.

90 *Aubrey: Brief Lives*, I, 37.

91 MS. Eng. Misc. d. 26, f. 70v.

Chapter 4

1 For Thomas Thorpe's dedications to his editions of Lucan, Epictetus, and Augustine, see Leona Rostenberg, "Thomas Thorpe: Publisher of 'Shakespeare's Sonnets,'" *The Papers of the Bibliographical Society of America*, 54 (First Quarter, 1960), 18–19, 29, 33–4.

2 *Shake-speares Sonnets* (1609), facsimile edn. (Menston: Scolar Press, 1970).

3 All quotations from the Sonnets are from *The Oxford Shakespeare: The Complete Sonnets and Poems*, ed. Colin Burrow (Oxford: Oxford University Press, 2002), and will be identified parenthetically by sonnet number.

4 Lukas Erne and Tamsin Badcoe, "Shakespeare and the Popularity of Poetry Books in Print, 1583–1622," *Review of English Studies*, 65 (2014), 33–57.

5 *A Collection of Poems, in Two Volumes; Being All the Miscellanies of Mr. William Shakespeare, Which Were Publish'd by Himself in the Year 1609, and Now Correctly Printed from Those Editions*, ed. B. Lintott (1711).

6 *A Collection of Poems, viz. I. Venus and Adonis. II. The Rape of Lucrece. III. The Passionate Pilgrim. IV. Sonnets to Sundry Notes of Musick. By Mr. William Shakespeare*, ed. B. Lintott (1709). For Lintott's and Gildon's publications of Shakespeare's poems as "*competing* editions," "both designed as sequels" to Rowe's 1709 edition, see Paul D. Cannan, "The 1709/11 Editions of Shakespeare's Poems," in Emma Depledge and Peter Kirwan, eds., *Canonising Shakespeare: Stationers and the Book Trade, 1640–1740* (Cambridge: Cambridge University Press, 2017), 172, 173.

7 Quoted by Cannan, "The 1709/11 Editions," 181.

8 For a discussion of five early sammelbands that include works by Shakespeare, see Jeffrey Todd Knight, *Bound to Read: Compilations, Collections, and the Making of Renaissance Literature* (Philadelphia: University of Pennsylvania Press, 2013), 70–84.

9   On the rarity of eighteenth-century type-facsimile, see David McKitterick, *Old Books, New Technologies: The Representation, Conservation and Transformation of Books since 1700* (Cambridge: Cambridge University Press, 2013). For the antiquarian appeal of Lintott's edition, see Cannan, "The 1709/11 Editions," 173–4, 185.

10 Capell's copy of Lintott's undated two-volumes-in-one octavo is held in the library of Trinity College, Cambridge (MS. Capell 4). As W. W. Greg's description of this copy specifies, "The volume apparently contains Capell's material for an edition of [Benson's] Poems." See *Catalogue of the Books Presented by Edward Capell to the Library of Trinity College in Cambridge* (Cambridge: Cambridge University Press, 1903), 165–6.

11 *Twenty of the Plays of Shakespeare, Being the Whole Number Printed in Quarto during His Life-time, or before the Restoration, Collated Where There Were Different Copies, and Publish'd from the Originals*, ed. George Steevens, 4 vols. (1766), I, 7.

12 *Twenty of the Plays of Shakespeare*, I, 13.

13 On the study of Old English throughout the eighteenth century spurred by George Hickes, see Rosemary Sweet, "Antiquaries and Antiquities in Eighteenth-Century England," *Eighteenth-Century Studies*, 34 (2001), 181–206.

14 *The Plays of William Shakspeare*, ed. Samuel Johnson and George Steevens, 15 vols. (1793), I, vii.

15 Malone published three editions of Shakespeare's 1609 Sonnets: *Supplement to the Edition of Shakespeare's Plays Published in 1778 by Samuel Johnson and George Steevens*, ed. Edmond Malone, 2 vols. (1780), I, 579–706; *The Plays and Poems of William Shakspeare*, ed. Edmond Malone, 10 vols. (1790), X, 189–317; and Malone–Boswell 1821, XX, 215–391. Except when otherwise noted, I quote from Malone–Boswell 1821. Page numbers to volume 20 of that edition will hereafter be given parenthetically in the text.

16 On the 43-play canon introduced by the second impression of Shakespeare's Third Folio, see Peter Kirwan, *Shakespeare and the Idea of Apocrypha: Negotiating the Boundaries of the Dramatic Canon* (Cambridge: Cambridge University Press, 2015), 18–28.

17 For Steevens's castigation of Malone for defiling his editorial instruments, particularly with sonnet 20, see Peter Stallybrass, "Editing as Cultural Formation: The Sexing of Shakespeare's Sonnets," in Marshall Brown, ed., *The Uses of Literary History* (Durham, NC: Duke University Press, 1995), 129–42.

18 See also Malone's defensive gloss on the poet's reference to himself as the "lover" of another man in sonnet 32. Malone–Boswell 1821, XX, 255–6 n. 8.

19 The suggestion that sonnet 145 puns on Anne Hathaway's name was first proposed by Stephen Daedalus in James Joyce's *Ulysses*. See Andrew Gurr, "Shakespeare's First Poem: Sonnet 145," *Essays in Criticism*, 21 (1971), 221–6.

20 For William Oldys's copy of Langbaine, see Chapter 1. Oldys notes his suspicion on p. 455 of his copy of Langbaine, held by the British Library (C.28.g.1). Oldys had been commissioned to write a new Life of Shakespeare by the bookseller Robert Walker, but the commission was returned at Oldys's death. See John Taylor's biographical notice on Oldys in *Records of My Life*, 2 vols. (London: Edward Bull, 1832), I, 28; and Paulina Kewes, "Shakespeare's Lives in Print, 1662–1821," in Robin Myers, Michael Harris, and Giles Mandelbrote, eds., *Lives in Print: Biography and the Book Trade from the Middle Ages to the 21st Century* (New Castle, DE: Oak Knoll Press, 2002), 65.

21 Oldys, according to Taylor, "frequently indulged his spleen in sarcasms against female inconstancy." See *Records of My Life*, 29.

22 For Malone's own romantic disappointment, see Peter Martin, *Edmond Malone, Shakespearean Scholar* (Cambridge: Cambridge University Press, 1995), 11–2, 16–7.

23 On the performative possibilities of the long dash in the printing of early modern playtexts, see Claire M. L. Bourne, *Typographies of Performance in Early Modern England* (Oxford: Oxford University Press, 2020), 106–8, 129–33.

24 Malone–Boswell 1821, IX, 413–14. Malone uses the same typographical marks in editing the jealous outbreaks of Leontes, Ford, and Posthumus.

25 On Malone's misconstrual of Shakespeare's bequest to his wife, see Lena Cowen Orlin, *The Private Life of William Shakespeare* (Oxford: Oxford University Press, 2021), 176, 188–95. For his limited understanding of seventeenth-century property laws and testamentary conventions, see 171–88, esp. 176–7.

26 As Boswell points out, in all four plays cited by Malone, jealousy proves delusional, "causeless and unjust," Malone-Boswell 1821, II, 309, n. 4.

27 In addition to his oversized gloss on sonnet 93, Malone's "conjecture" can be found in the following: the note on Oldys's copy of Langbaine, cited in n. 20 above, interleaf to p. 455; *An Inquiry into the Authenticity of Certain Miscellaneous Papers and Legal Instruments* (1796), 282–3; and Malone–Boswell 1821, II, 607 n. 6.

28 Alexander Dyce, "Memoir of Shakespeare," in *The Poems of Shakespeare*, ed. Alexander Dyce (London: Pickering, 1832), xi.

29 According to Schoenbaum, Malone's note to sonnet 93 proved "more influential than any other single statement [Malone] would ever make." See *Shakespeare's Lives*, 120.

30 See A. D. Harvey, "Prosecutions for Sodomy in England at the Beginning of the Nineteenth Century," *The Historical Journal*, 21 (1978), 939.

31 For Malone's influence on subsequent editions of the Sonnets into the twentieth century, see *A New Variorum Edition of Shakespeare: The Sonnets*, ed. Hyder Edward Rollins, 2 vols. (Philadelphia: J. B. Lippincott & Co., 1944), I, 38–9.

32 William Wordsworth, "Essay, Supplementary to the Preface," in *Poems by William Wordsworth: Including Lyrical Ballads, and the Miscellaneous Pieces of the Author*, 2 vols. (London: Printed for Longman, Hurst, Rees, Orme, and Brown, 1815), I, 352.

33 Wordsworth, "Scorn Not the Sonnet," as discussed by Jonathan Bate in *The Genius of Shakespeare* (London: Picador, 1997), 37.

34 *The Sonnets of William Shakspere*, ed. Edward Dowden (London: C. K. Paul & Co., 1881), xxxii.

35 *Shakespeare's Sonnets Reconsidered: and in Part Rearranged with Introductory Chapters, Notes, and a Reprint of the Original 1609 Edition*, ed. Samuel Butler (London: Longmans, Green & Co., 1899).

36 In their recent edition of the Sonnets, Paul Edmondson and Stanley Wells have also arranged the poems in the order in which they have estimated them to have been written, "from some time before 1582 up to 1613." As they stress, their dating across a span of almost thirty years precludes the search for a biographical narrative. Yet many of the sonnets remain for them "deeply personal poems written out of Shakespeare's own experience." See *All the Sonnets of Shakespeare* (Cambridge: Cambridge University Press, 2020), 25, 32.

37 Letter from Malone to Thomas Warton, August 17, 1789, quoted by Martin, *Edmond Malone*, 126.

38 On the eighteenth-century overlap of pocketbooks with diaries, see Sandro Jung, "Illustrated Pocket Diaries and the Commodification of Culture," *Eighteenth-Century Life*, 37 (2013), 53–84.

39 See H. R. Woudhuysen, "Writing-Tables and Table-Books," *The Electronic British Library Journal* (2004), 3.5–8; and Peter Stallybrass et al., "Hamlet's Tables and the Technologies of Writing in Renaissance England," *Shakespeare Quarterly*, 55 (Winter 2004), 379–419.

40 *Shakespeare's Sonnets*, ed. Katherine Duncan-Jones, rev. edn., Arden Shakespeare (London: Bloomsbury, 2010), 42. First printed in 1997, this edition was revised in 2010 and reprinted every year from 2013 up to 2019.

41 For editions of the Sonnets which reference the 1640 *Poems* as the "second edition" of the 1609 *Sonnets*, see Margreta de Grazia, "The First Reader of Shake-speares Sonnets," in Leonard Barkan, Brian Cormack, and Sean Keilen, eds., *The Forms of Renaissance Thought: New Essays in Literature and Culture* (New York: Palgrave Macmillan, 2009), 86–7, 103 n. 3. In Jane Kingsley-Smith's extensive history of the reception of Shakespeare's Sonnets, she oddly terms the 1640 *Poems* "the first printed edition of the Sonnets"; see *The Afterlife of Shakespeare's Sonnets* (Cambridge: Cambridge University Press, 2019), 66. Only by identifying Benson's 1640 *Poems* as an edition of Thorpe's 1609 Sonnets is she able to argue for an unbroken history of the Sonnets' presence in print from 1609 up through the eighteenth century and beyond.

42 For a table of the 759 textual variants between the 1640 *Poems* and the 1609 *Sonnets*, see the appendix to Carl D. Atkins, "The Importance of Compositorial Error and Variation to the Emendation of Shakespeare's Texts: A Bibliographic Analysis of Benson's 1640 Text of Shakespeare's Sonnets," *Studies in Philology*, 104 (Summer 2007), 306–39.

43 For the contents and sources of Benson's 1640 *Poems*, see Appendix 1 and 2 in Cathy Shrank, "Reading Shakespeare's Sonnets: John Benson and the 1640 Poems," *Shakespeare*, 5 (2009), 282–91.

44 *A New Variorum Edition of Shakespeare: The Sonnets*, II, 18, 20.

45 Versions of sonnets 138 and 144 appear as the first two poems of the 1599 *The Passionate Pilgrim*, reproduced in *The Complete Sonnets and Poems*, ed. Burrow, 341–2. For a discussion of *The Passionate Pilgrim* as a discrete edition meriting critical attention, see Faith D. Acker, *First Readers of Shakespeare's Sonnets, 1590–1790* (London: Routledge, 2020), 10–30.

46 As Cathy Shrank has concluded, "Benson's 1640 *Poems* is designed as a miscellany," "Reading Shakespeare's Sonnets," 278. According to Megan Heffernan, Thomas Warton was the first to refer to Tottel's compilation as a "miscellany" in 1781. See *Making the Miscellany: Poetry, Print, and the History of the Book in Early Modern England* (Philadelphia: University of Pennsylvania Press, 2021), 8.

47 For a legal defense of Benson's practices, see Josephine Waters Bennett, "Benson's Alleged Piracy of *Shake-speares Sonnets* and of Some of Jonson's Works," *Studies in Bibliography*, 21 (1968), 235–48.

48 *The Works of Mr. William Shakespear: Volume the Seventh*, ed. Charles Gildon (1710). For Lintott's edition, see n. 5 above.

49 Colin Burrow, "Life and Work in Shakespeare's Poems," The British Academy Chatterton Lecture, *Proceedings of the British Academy*, 97 (1997), 15–50, at 17. William Jaggard considers them two separate works with separate histories of publication; see *Shakespeare Bibliography* (1911; repr., London: Dawsons of Pall Mall, 1971), 435.

50 "To the Reader," in *Poems: Written by Wil. Shake-speare. Gent.*, n.p.

51 Ovid, *Metamorphoses*, trans. Frank Justus Miller, 2 vols. (Cambridge, MA: Harvard University Press, 1951), II,15. 497–546.

52 Jean-Christophe Mayer, "Transmission as Appropriation: The Early Reception of John Benson's Edition of Shakespeare's Poems (1640)," *Journal of Early Modern Studies*, 5 (2016), 420–21. On the manuscript practices of extracting, collecting, reassembling, and retitling Shakespeare's Sonnets, see also Sasha Roberts, *Reading Shakespeare's Poems in Early Modern England* (Basingstoke: Palgrave Macmillan, 2003), 143–90; and Faith D. Acker, "Manuscript Precedents for Editorial Practices in John Benson's *Poems: Written by Wil. Shake-Speare. Gent.*," *Shakespeare Quarterly*, 71 (Spring 2020), 1–24.

53 Jason Scott-Warren, "Commonplacing and Originality: Reading Francis Meres," *The Review of English Studies*, 68 (2017), 902–23.

54 Bennett, "Benson's Alleged Piracy," 237, 246–7.

55 Compare the headings culled by Emma Smith from readers' marks in the First Folio. *Shakespeare's First Folio: The Biography* (New York: Oxford University Press, 2016), 140–1.

56 On Benson's modeling of the composite poem he titles "A Valediction" on the model of Donne's valedictions, see Heffernan, *Making the Miscellany*, 204–11.

57 Peter Beal, *Index of English Literary Manuscripts: 1450–1625* (London: Mansell, 1980), I, pt. 2, 552–4.

58 On the appeal of this sonnet as a Cavalier seduction lyric, see *Shakespeare's Sonnets*, ed. Duncan-Jones, 453.

59 Gary Taylor, "Some Manuscripts of Shakespeare's Sonnets," *Bulletin of the John Rylands Library*, 68 (1985), 212.

60 Mayer, "Transmission as Appropriation," 411–8.

61 Roberts, *Reading Shakespeare's Poems*, 167–9.

62 On the frequency with which the epigrammatic "point" or "summe" of a sonnet is captured in its couplet and thereby made available for wide dispersal, see Jessica Rosenberg, *Botanical Poetics: Early Modern Plant Books and the Husbandry of Print*, (Philadelphia: University of Pennsylvania Press, 2022), 243–52.

63 As cited by Roberts, *Reading Shakespeare's Poems*, 7, 200 n. 17.

64 See Mayer, "Transmission as Appropriation," 418–20.

65 For the two miscellanies as well as John Suckling's play, see Kingsley-Smith, *The Afterlife of Shakespeare's Sonnets*, 73–9, 89–93.

66 Gildon, "Critical Remarks," in *The Works of Mr. William Shakespear: Volume the Seventh*, 447. The 1640 *Poems* are first published with the plays in Gildon's "volume the seventh," an addendum to Rowe's 1709 six-volume edition. They are published in the edition proper in Rowe's second edition, *The Works of Mr. William Shakespear, in Nine Volumes* (1714), IX, 101–235. His [Shakespeare's] *Miscellany Poems*, in *The Works of Mr. William Shakespear: Volume the Seventh*, 111–256.

67 As Stephen Orgel has pointed out, the Sonnets were not routinely included in editions of Shakespeare's collected or complete works until well into the twentieth century. See "The Desire and Pursuit of the Whole," *Shakespeare Quarterly*, 58 (Fall 2007), 291–2.

68 Aleida Auld takes both Lintott's and Gildon's reference to Shakespeare's mistress as support for her thesis that the 1609 *Sonnets* were read biographically before Malone's edition. See "Biographical Reconfigurations of Shakespeare's Sonnets: John Benson, Charles Gildon, and the Catullan Epigram," *Shakespeare*, 18 (2022), 197–222.

69 On the rivalry between these two publications, "both designed as sequels to the Tonson-Rowe edition," see Cannan, "The 1709/11 Editions," 171–86, at 173; and Peter Holland, introduction to *The Works of Mr. William Shakespear, edited by Nicholas Rowe, 1709*, 7 vols. (London: Pickering and Chatto, 1999), I, xxiv–xxvi. On both Lintott's and Gildon's innovative use of "miscellany" for Shakespeare's poems, see Heffernan, *Making the Miscellany*, 214. For the Copyright Act of 1710 as "the precipitating force" behind this rivalry, see Burrow, "Life and Work in Shakespeare's Poems," 17.

70 Nicholas Rowe, *Some Account of the Life, &c. of Mr. William Shakespear*, in *The Works of Mr. William Shakespear*, ed. Nicholas Rowe, 6 vols. (1709), I, xl.

71 *Daily Courant*, June 24, 1709, quoted by Cannan, "The 1709/11 Editions," 175.

72 Rowe's immediate editorial successors, Lewis Theobald and William Warburton, both contemplated adding Benson's 1640 *Poems* to their editions of Shakespeare. See *A New Variorum Edition of Shakespeare: The Sonnets*, II, 30, 334, 605. It appears that Edward Capell intended the same, see n. 10 above.

73 Giles E. Dawson, *Four Centuries of Shakespeare Publishing*, as cited in Andrew Murphy, *Shakespeare in Print: A History and Chronology of Shakespeare Publishing* (Cambridge: Cambridge University Press, 2003), 63. See also Cannan, "Early Shakespeare Criticism, Charles Gildon, and the Making of Shakespeare the Playwright-Poet," *Modern Philology*, 102 (August 2004), 35–55.

74 Gildon, "Critical Remarks," in *The Works of Mr. William Shakespear: Volume the Seventh*, 257–464, at 347.

75 Gildon, "Critical Remarks," 457. On the twinning of the epigram and sonnet forms in the Renaissance, see Rosalie Colie, *Shakespeare's Living Art* (Princeton, NJ: Princeton University Press, 1974), 75.

76 Gildon, "Critical Remarks," 463.

77 Gildon, "An Essay on the Art, Rise and Progress of the Stage," in *The Works of Mr. William Shakespear: Volume the Seventh*, iv, v. For the foregrounding of "detachable Shakespeare," from the "shining passages" of Pope's 1723 edition to the beauties of William Dodd's 1752 *The Beauties of Shakespeare*, see Brean Hammond, "Pope's Shakespeare and Poetic Quotation," in Julie Maxwell and Kate Rumbold, eds., *Shakespeare and Quotation* (Cambridge: Cambridge University Press, 2018), 107–19.

78 Gildon, "Critical Remarks," 467, 471.

79 Samuel Johnson, preface to *The Plays of William Shakespeare*, ed. Samuel Johnson, 8 vols. (1765), I, xl.

80 Samuel Johnson, *A Dictionary of the English Language: in which the Words Are Deduced from Their Originals, and Illustrated in Their Different Significations by Examples from the Best Writers*, 2 vols. (1755), I, n.p.

81 Quotations from Shakespeare similarly have dominated the *OED*, "so that his works are the source of 32868 quotations in the OED—about 1.8% of the total,

and more than twice as many as from any other named author." See John Considine, "Literary Classics in OED Quotation Evidence," *Review of English Studies*, 60 (2009), 620–38, at 621.

82 First published anonymously in the preliminaries to *Mr. William Shakespeares Comedies, Histories, and Tragedies* (1632), A5r, "An Epitaph" subsequently appeared in both John Benson's *Poems* (1640), K8r–v, and in *Poems of Mr. John Milton, Both English and Latin, Compos'd at Several Times* (1645), 27.

83 I quote the poem from the 1645 version, entitled "On Shakespeare. 1630," in *The Complete Works of John Milton, Vol. 3: The Shorter Poems*, ed. Barbara Kiefer Lewalski and Estelle Haan (Oxford: Oxford University Press, 2012), 25.

84 *Milton: The Shorter Poems*, 371.

85 The maxims were transcribed by the fifth-century compiler John Stobaeus in his four-book anthology of Greek extracts, printed in Latin in the sixteenth and seventeenth centuries in two books, a key source of aphorisms throughout the Renaissance. On Milton's use of Stobaeus, see Joshua Scodel, "Paradise Lost and Classical Ideals of Pleasurable Restraint," *Comparative Literature*, 48 (1996), 216.

86 Quintilian, *The Orator's Education*, ed. and trans. Donald A. Russell, 5 vols. (Cambridge, MA: Harvard University Press, 2001), 1.1.35–6. The Delphic oracular maxims could be seen as the classical counterpart to the Mosaic commandments, also to be "written ... not in tables of stone, but in fleshly tables of the heart" (2 Corinthians 3:3).

87 For the discovery and identification of this copy as Milton's, see Claire M. L. Bourne and Jason Scott-Warren, "'thy unvalued Booke': John Milton's Copy of the Shakespeare First Folio," *Milton Quarterly* (forthcoming). I wish to thank the authors for sharing their essay with me before publication.

88 *The Complete Sonnets and Poems*, ed. Burrow, 542 n. 9. For evidence of Milton's knowledge of the Sonnets, see Kingsley-Smith, *The Afterlife of Shakespeare's Sonnets*, 79–86.

89 For a trenchant challenge to this longstanding assumption, see Lukas Erne, *Shakespeare as Literary Dramatist* (Cambridge: Cambridge University Press, 2003), esp. 30–5.

90 Alexander Pope, *The First Epistle of the Second Book of Horace, Imitated* (1737), 9.

91 Johnson, preface to *The Plays of William Shakespeare* (1765), I, xlv.

92 Johnson may have read them at a later point, in the 1766 publication of Shakespearean quartos by his co-editor, George Steevens, *Twenty of the Plays of Shakespeare*. See R. Carter Hailey, "'This instance will not do': George Steevens, Shakespeare, and the Revision(s) of Johnson's *Dictionary*," *Studies in Bibliography*, 54 (2001), 243–64.

93 For good reason to rename these sonnets "the preservation sonnets," see Aaron Kunin, "Shakespeare's Preservation Fantasy," *PMLA*, 124 (2009), 92–106.

94 As noted by John Kerrigan in his edition of *The Sonnets and a Lover's Complaint* (London: Harmondsworth, 1986), 241.

95 Horace, *Odes* in *Odes and Epodes*, ed. and trans. Niall Rudd (Cambridge, MA: Harvard University Press, 2004), 3.30.1–7.

96 Ovid, *The. XV. Bookes of P. Ouidius Naso, Entytuled Metamorphosis*, trans. Arthur Golding (1567), 200.

97 August Wilhelm von Schlegel, *A Course of Lectures on Dramatic Art and Literature*, trans. John Black, 2 vols. (London: Printed for Baldwin, Cradock, and Joy, 1815), II, 113.

98 Malone–Boswell 1821, XX, 217.

99 By Paul Ramsey's estimate, 22.5 percent of all males in Shakespeare's England were named William. See *Fickle Glass: A Study of Shakespeare's Sonnets* (New York: AMS Press, 1979), 23.

100 See Stephen Booth's commentary on "will" in sonnets 135 and 136 in his edition of *Shakespeare's Sonnets* (1997; repr., New Haven, CT: Yale University Press, 2000), 466, (d) and (e).

101 According to Edmondson and Wells, 84 of the 154 sonnets "could be addressed to either a male or female," and not necessarily the same male or female. See their "Table 2: The Direction of Shakespeare's Sonnets," in *All the Sonnets of Shakespeare*, 28–9.

102 Meres, *Palladis Tamia*, 282v–r.

Acknowledgments

The subject of this book had long been in the back of my mind and would be there still if not for the invitation by Oxford University Press to deliver the Oxford Wells Shakespeare Lectures in the autumn of 2018. I am grateful to OUP for this occasion, and to the Shakespearean in whose honor the lecture series was established. The Shakespeare I know is the one Stanley Wells has edited, elucidated, contextualized, and brought to life during his long and illustrious career.

I also thank the members of the Oxford English Faculty who nominated me for the series, as well as those who attended and responded to the lectures, among them Colin Burrow, Lorna Hutson, Laurie Maguire, Helen Small, Emma Smith, and especially Bart van Es who presided over the series.

The interval between the delivery of the lectures and their publication gave me time to ponder and refine their content. I was also able to absorb the discerning comments of the four readers of the book in typescript. My deep thanks to Peter Holland, Lucy Munro, Peter Stallybrass, and Tiffany Stern.

The expertise of several scholars informed specific areas of the book. Kate Bennett dispensed with knowledge as brilliantly and generously in person as she has in her edition of Aubrey's *Brief Lives*. Kathryn James opened me to the pathologies of the antiquarian. Jessica Rosenberg's centrifugal reading of the Sonnets helped liberate my own. Megan Cook provided parallels from the construction of Chaucer's life. Ian Gadd addressed queries on early printing practices. Finally, and as always, my thanks to Peter Stallybrass, for his gift of making sparks fly.

For conversations over the years about the quiddities of authorship and biography, I thank Crystal Bartolovich, Brian Cummings, Juliet Fleming, Jay Grossman, Richard Holmes, Gabriel Josipovici, Louisa Lane Fox, Jeff Masten, Laurie Shannon, Bronwyn Wallace, and above all, Austin Zeiderman.

For help in preparing the typescript for publication, I have Alison Howard to thank. Eleanor Collins patiently saw the book through to completion, with the assistance of Aimee Wright and Mark Ajin Millet, and Amanda Brown spared me the labor of obtaining images and permissions, largely through the courtesy of the Bodleian Libraries. I am grateful to the Weston Library and its librarians for access to its Special Collections, and to their curator, Michael Webb, for tracking down elusive manuscripts.

Bibliography

Editions of Shakespeare

Complete Works

Mr. William Shakespeares Comedies, Histories, & Tragedies, ed. John Heminges and Henry Condell (1623).

Mr. William Shakespeares Comedies, Histories, and Tragedies, ed. John Heminges and Henry Condell (1632).

The Works of Mr. William Shakespear, ed. Nicholas Rowe, 6 vols. (1709).

The Works of Mr. William Shakespear: Volume the Seventh: Containing Venus and Adonis ... with Critical Remarks on His Plays, etc., to which is Prefix'd an Essay on the Art, Rise and Progress of the Stage in Greece, Rome and England, ed. Charles Gildon (1710).

The Works of Mr. William Shakespear, ed. Nicholas Rowe, 9 vols. (1714).

The Works of Shakespear, ed. Alexander Pope, 6 vols. (1725).

The Works of Shakespeare, ed. Lewis Theobald, 7 vols. (1733).

The Plays of William Shakespeare, ed. Samuel Johnson, 8 vols. (1765).

Twenty of the Plays of Shakespeare, Being the Whole Number Printed in Quarto during His Life-time, or before the Restoration, Collated Where There Were Different Copies, and Publish'd from the Originals, ed. George Steevens, 4 vols. (1766).

Mr. William Shakespeare, His Comedies, Histories, and Tragedies, ed. Edward Capell (1767).

The Plays of William Shakespeare, ed. Samuel Johnson and George Steevens, 10 vols. (1778).

Supplement to the Edition of Shakspeare's Plays Published in 1778 by Samuel Johnson and George Steevens, ed. Edmond Malone, 2 vols. (1780).

The Plays of William Shakespeare, ed. Samuel Johnson, George Steevens, and Isaac Reed, 10 vols. (1785).

The Plays and Poems of William Shakspeare, ed. Edmond Malone, 10 vols. (1790).

The Plays of William Shakspeare, ed. Samuel Johnson and George Steevens, 15 vols. (1793).

The Plays and Poems of William Shakspeare, ed. Edmond Malone and James Boswell, 21 vols. (London: F. C. and J. Rivington [etc.], 1821).

The Dramatic Works of Shakespeare, ed. Alexander Chalmers (London: William Pickering, 1826).

Shakspere's Werke. Herausgegeben und erklärt von N. Delius, ed. Nikolaus Delius, 7 vols. (Elberfeld: L. Friderichs, 1854–61).

The Pictorial Edition of the Works of Shakspere, ed. Charles Knight, 2nd edn., 2 vols. (London: G. Routledge & Sons, 1867).

The Leopold Shakespeare: The Poet's Works in Chronological Order, from the Text of Professor Delius (London: Cassell, Petter, & Galpin, 1877).

The Complete Works of William Shakespeare, ed. Sidney Lee (New York: Harper & Brothers, 1906–8).

The Oxford Shakespeare: The Complete Works, ed. Stanley Wells, Gary Taylor, John Jowett, and William Montgomery, 2nd edn. (Oxford: Oxford University Press, 2005).

Single Plays

King Henry VI, Part Three, ed. John D. Cox and Eric Rasmussen, Arden Shakespeare, 3rd ser. (London: Bloomsbury, 2001).

Sir Thomas More, ed. John Jowett, Arden Shakespeare, 3rd ser. (London: Bloomsbury, 2011).

Titus Andronicus, ed. Jonathan Bate, rev. edn., Arden Shakespeare, 3rd ser. (London: Bloomsbury, 2018).

Sonnets

Shake-speares Sonnets, 1609, facsimile edn. (Menston: Scolar Press, 1970).

Poems: Written by Wil. Shake-speare. Gent., ed. John Benson (1640).

A Collection of Poems, viz. I. Venus and Adonis. II. The Rape of Lucrece. III. The Passionate Pilgrim. IV. Sonnets to Sundry Notes of Musick. By Mr. William Shakespeare, ed. B. Lintott (1709).

A Collection of Poems, in Two Volumes; Being All the Miscellanies of Mr. William Shakespeare, Which Were Publish'd by Himself in the Year 1609, and Now Correctly Printed from Those Editions, ed. B. Lintott (1711).

The Sonnets of William Shakspere, ed. Edward Dowden (London: C. K. Paul & Co., 1881).

Shakespeare's Sonnets Reconsidered: And in Part Rearranged with Introductory Chapters, Notes, and a Reprint of the Original 1609 Edition, ed. Samuel Butler (London: Longmans, Green, & Co., 1899).

A New Variorum Edition of Shakespeare: The Sonnets, ed. Hyder Edward Rollins, 2 vols. (Philadelphia & London: J. B. Lippincott & Co., 1944).

The Sonnets and a Lover's Complaint, ed. John Kerrigan (London: Harmondsworth, 1986).

Shakespeare's Sonnets, ed. Stephen Booth (1977; repr., New Haven, CT: Yale University Press, 2000).

The Oxford Shakespeare: The Complete Sonnets and Poems, ed. Colin Burrow (Oxford: Oxford University Press, 2002).

Shakespeare's Sonnets, ed. Katherine Duncan-Jones, rev. edn., Arden Shakespeare (London: Bloomsbury, 2010).

All the Sonnets of Shakespeare, ed. Paul Edmondson and Stanley Wells (Cambridge: Cambridge University Press, 2020).

Primary and Secondary Sources

Acker, Faith D., *First Readers of Shakespeare's Sonnets, 1590–1790* (London: Routledge, 2020).

Acker, Faith D., "Manuscript Precedents for Editorial Practices in John Benson's *Poems: Written by Wil. Shake-Speare. Gent.*," *Shakespeare Quarterly*, 71 (Spring 2020), 1–24.

Anonymous, *The Three Parnassus Plays*, ed. J. B. Leishman (London: Ivor Nicholson & Watson, 1949).

Atkins, Carl D., "The Importance of Compositorial Error and Variation to the Emendation of Shakespeare's Texts: A Bibliographic Analysis of Benson's 1640 Text of Shakespeare's Sonnets," *Studies in Philology*, 104(Summer 2007), 306–39.

Aubrey, John, *"Brief Lives," Chiefly of Contemporaries, Set Down by John Aubrey, between the Years 1669 and 1696*, ed. Andrew Clark, 2 vols. (Oxford: Clarendon Press, 1898).

Aubrey, John, *Brief Lives with An Apparatus for the Lives of Our English Mathematical Writers*, ed. Kate Bennett, 2 vols. (Oxford: Oxford University Press, 2015).

Auld, Aleida, "Biographical Reconfigurations of Shakespeare's Sonnets: John Benson, Charles Gildon, and the Catullan Epigram," *Shakespeare*, 18 (2022), 197–222.

Baldwin, T. W., *William Shakspere's Small Latine and Lesse Greeke*, 2 vols. (Urbana: University of Illinois Press, 1944).

Bate, Jonathan, *The Genius of Shakespeare* (London: Picador, 1997).

Beal, Peter, *Index of English Literary Manuscripts: 1450–1625* (London: Mansell, 1980).

Bennett, Josephine Waters, "Benson's Alleged Piracy of *Shake-speares Sonnets* and of Some of Jonson's Works," *Studies in Bibliography*, 21 (1968), 235–48.

Bennett, Kate, "Shakespeare's Monument at Stratford: A New Seventeenth-Century Account," *Notes and Queries*, 47 (2000), 464.

Bennett, Kate, "John Aubrey and the Printed Book," *Huntington Library Quarterly*, 76 (2013), 393–411.

Bennett, Kate, "General Introduction," in *John Aubrey: Brief Lives with An Apparatus for the Lives of Our English Mathematical Writers*, ed. Kate Bennett, 2 vols. (Oxford: Oxford University Press, 2015).

Blair, Hugh, *Lectures on Rhetoric and Belles Lettres*, 2 vols. (1783).

Bland, Mark, "Francis Beaumont's Verse Letters to Ben Jonson and 'The Mermaid Club,'" in Peter Beal and A. S. G. Edwards, eds., *Scribes and Transmission in English Manuscripts 1400–1700*, English Manuscript Studies 1100–1700 12 (London: British Library, 2005).

Boase, T. S. R., "Illustrations of Shakespeare's Plays in the Seventeenth and Eighteenth Centuries," *Journal of the Warburg and Courtauld Institutes*, 10 (1947), 83–108.

Boswell, James, *The Life of Samuel Johnson* (1791).

Bourne, Claire M. L., *Typographies of Performance* (Oxford: Oxford University Press, 2020).

Bourne, Claire M. L., and Jason Scott-Warren, "'thy unvalued Booke': John Milton's Copy of the Shakespeare First Folio," *Milton Quarterly*, 56 (2022): 1–85.

Burrow, Colin, "Life and Work in Shakespeare's Poems," The British Academy Chatterton Lecture, *Proceedings of the British Academy*, 97 (1997), 15–50.

Cannan, Paul D., "Early Shakespeare Criticism, Charles Gildon, and the Making of Shakespeare the Playwright-Poet," *Modern Philology*, 102 (August 2004), 35–55.

Cannan, Paul D., "The 1709/11 Editions of Shakespeare's Poems," in Emma Depledge and Peter Kirwan, eds., *Canonising Shakespeare: Stationers and the Book Trade, 1640–1740* (Cambridge: Cambridge University Press, 2017), 171–86.

Capell, Edward, *Notes and Various Readings*, 3 vols. (1779–83).

Caulfield, James, *An Enquiry into the Conduct of Edmond Malone, Concerning the Manuscript Papers of John Aubrey* (1797).

Caulfield, James, *The Oxford Cabinet; Consisting of Engravings from Original Pictures, in the Ashmolean Museum, and Other Public and Private Collections; with Biographical Anecdotes, by John Aubrey, F. R. S.* (1797).

Chartier, Roger, *The Author's Hand and the Printer's Mind: Transformations of the Written Word in Early Modern Europe* (Oxford: Polity Press, 2013).

Chettle, Henry, and Robert Greene, *Greene's Groatsworth of Wit: Bought with a Million of Repentance*, ed. D. Allen Carroll (New York: Medieval & Renaissance Texts & Studies, 1994).

Coleridge, Samuel Taylor, *Biographia Literaria; or, Biographical Sketches of My Literary Life*, 2 vols. (London: Rest Fenner, 1817).

Coleridge, Samuel Taylor, *The Literary Remains of Samuel Taylor Coleridge*, 2 vols. (London: William Pickering, 1836).

Coleridge, Samuel Taylor, *Notes and Lectures upon Shakespeare and Some of the Old Poets and Dramatists* (London: William Pickering, 1849).

Colie, Rosalie, *Shakespeare's Living Art* (Princeton, NJ: Princeton University Press, 1974).

Collier, John Payne, *Reasons for a New Edition of Shakespeare's Works* (London: Whittaker, 1841).

Collings, E., "Ghosts in the Archive: Edmond Malone, Craven Ord, and the Missing Texts of Henry Herbert's Office-Book," *The Critical Quarterly*, 55 (2013), 30–41.

Considine, John, "Literary Classics in OED Quotation Evidence," *Review of English Studies*, 60 (2009), 620–38.

Corn, Alfred, "Shakespeare's Epitaph," *Hudson Review*, 64 (2011), 295–303.

de Grazia, Margreta, *Shakespeare Verbatim: The Reproduction of Authenticity and the 1790 Apparatus* (Oxford: Oxford University Press, 1991).

de Grazia, Margreta, *"Hamlet" without Hamlet* (Cambridge: Cambridge University Press, 2007).

de Grazia, Margreta, "The First Reader of *Shake-speares Sonnets*," in Leonard Barkan, Bradin Cormack, and Sean Keilen, eds., *The Forms of Renaissance Thought: New Essays in Literature and Culture* (New York: Palgrave Macmillan, 2008), 86–106.

de Grazia, Margreta, "Shakespeare's Timeline," *Shakespeare Quarterly*, 65 (Winter 2014), 379–98.

de Grazia, Margreta, "Shakespeare's Anecdotal Character," *Shakespeare Survey*, 68 (2015), 1–14.

de Grazia, Margreta, *Four Shakespearean Period Pieces* (Chicago: University of Chicago Press, 2021).

Donaldson, Ian, "Life of Ben Jonson," in *The Cambridge Edition of the Works of Ben Jonson*. Online (Cambridge: Cambridge University Press, 2014).

Dowden, Edward, *Shakspere* (New York: D. Appleton, 1878).

Dowden, Edward, *Shakspere: A Critical Study of His Mind and Art*, 3rd edn. (New York: Harper & Brothers, 1881).

Dryden, John, *The Tempest, or The Enchanted Island* (1670).

Dryden, John, *Troilus and Cressida, or, Truth Found Too Late ... to which is Prefix'd, a Preface Containing the Grounds of Criticism in Tragedy* (1679).

Dryden, John, *King Arthur: or, The British Worthy. A Dramatick Opera* (1691).

Dryden, John, *The Critical and Miscellaneous Prose Works of John Dryden*, ed. Edmond Malone, 4 vols. (London: T. Cadell, Jr. and W. Davies, 1800).

Dugdale, William, *The Antiquities of Warwickshire Illustrated* (1656).

Dyce, Alexander, "Memoir of Shakespeare," in *The Poems of Shakespeare*, ed. Alexander Dyce (London: Pickering, 1832), i–lxxvii.

Erne, Lukas, *Shakespeare as Literary Dramatist* (Cambridge: Cambridge University Press, 2003).

Erne, Lukas, and Tamsin Badcoe, "Shakespeare and the Popularity of Poetry Books in Print, 1583–1622," *Review of English Studies*, 65 (2014), 33–57.

Euripides, *Cyclops. Alcestis. Medea*, ed. and trans. David Kovacs (Cambridge, MA: Harvard University Press, 1994).

Farmer, Richard, *An Essay on the Learning of Shakespeare: Addressed to Joseph Cradock, Esq; The Second Edition, with Large Additions* (1767).

Fuller, Thomas, *The History of the Worthies of England*, ed. P. Austin Nuttall, 3 vols. (New York: AMS Press, 1965).

Furnivall, F. J., "The Founder's Prospectus," in *The New Shakspere Society's Transactions* (London: N. Trübner & Co., 1874), I, 6–10.

Galey, Alan, *The Shakespearean Archive: Experiments in New Media from the Renaissance to Postmodernity* (Cambridge: Cambridge University Press, 2014).

Goldsmith, Oliver, *Poems and Plays by Oliver Goldsmith, M.B., to which is Prefixed the Life of the Author* (1780).

Greenblatt, Stephen, *Shakespeare's Freedom* (Chicago: University of Chicago Press, 2010).

Greenblatt, Stephen, "The Traces of Shakespeare's Life," in Margreta de Grazia and Stanley Wells, eds., *The New Cambridge Companion to Shakespeare* (Cambridge: Cambridge University Press, 2010), 1–14.

Greg, W. W. (ed.), *Catalogue of the Books Presented by Edward Capell to the Library of Trinity College in Cambridge* (Cambridge: Cambridge University Press, 1903).

Gurr, Andrew, "Shakespeare's First Poem: Sonnet 145," *Essays in Criticism*, 21 (1971), 221–26.

Hailey, R. Carter, "'This instance will not do': George Steevens, Shakespeare, and the Revision(s) of Johnson's *Dictionary*," *Studies in Bibliography*, 54 (2001), 243–64.

Hamm, Robert B., Jr., "Rowe's Shakespeare (1709) and the Tonson House Style," *College Literature*, 31 (2004), 179–205.

Hammond, Brean, "Pope's Shakespeare and Poetic Quotation," in Julie Maxwell and Kate Rumbold, eds., *Shakespeare and Quotation* (Cambridge: Cambridge University Press, 2018), 107–19.

Han, Younglim, *Romantic Shakespeare: From Stage to Page* (Cranbury, NJ: Fairleigh Dickinson University Press, 2001).

Harvey, A. D., "Prosecutions for Sodomy in England at the Beginning of the Nineteenth Century," *The Historical Journal*, 21 (1978), 939–48.

Heavey, Katherine, "'An infant of the house of York': Medea and Absyrtus in Shakespeare's First Tetralogy," *Comparative Drama*, 50 (Summer & Fall 2016), 233–48.

Heffernan, Megan, "Turning Sonnets into Poems: Textual Affect and John Benson's Metaphysical Shakespeare," *Shakespeare Quarterly*, 64 (Spring 2013), 71–98.

Heffernan, Megan, *Making the Miscellany: Poetry, Print, and the History of the Book in Early Modern England* (Philadelphia: University of Pennsylvania Press, 2021).

Holland, Peter, introduction to *The Works of Mr. William Shakespear, edited by Nicholas Rowe*, 7 vols. (London: Pickering & Chatto, 1999).

Hooks, Adam G., "Making Histories; or, Shakespeare's Ring," in Heidi Brayman Hackel, Jesse M. Lander, and Zachary Lesser, eds., *The Book in History, the Book as History: New Intersections of the Material Text* (New Haven, CT: Yale University Press, 2016), 345–51.

Hooks, Adam G., *Selling Shakespeare: Biography, Bibliography, and the Book Trade* (Cambridge: Cambridge University Press, 2016).

Horace, *Odes and Epodes*, ed. and trans. Niall Rudd (Cambridge, MA: Harvard University Press, 2004).

Hurdis, James, *Cursory Remarks upon the Arrangement of the Plays of Shakespear Occasioned by Reading Mr. Malone's Essay on the Chronological Order of Those Celebrated Pieces* (1792).

Ide, Arata, "John Fletcher of Corpus Christi College: New Records of His Early Years," *Early Theatre*, 13 (2010), 63–77.

Ireland, Samuel, *Miscellaneous Papers and Legal Instruments under the Hand and Seal of W. Shakespeare: Including the Tragedy of King Lear, and a Small Fragment of Hamlet, from the Original MSS. in the Possession of Samuel Ireland, of Norfolk Street* (1796).

Ireland, William-Henry, *The Confessions of William-Henry Ireland: Containing the Particulars of His Fabrication of the Shakspeare Manuscripts* (London: Ellerton and Byworth, for T. Goddard, 1805).

Jaggard, William, *Shakespeare Bibliography* (1911; repr., London: Dawsons of Pall Mall, 1971).

James, Kathryn, *English Paleography and Manuscript Culture, 1500–1800* (New Haven, CT: Yale University Press, 2020).

Johnson, Samuel, *A Dictionary of the English Language: in which the Words Are Deduced from Their Originals, and Illustrated in Their Different Significations by Examples from the Best Writers ...*, 2 vols. (1755).

Jonson, Ben, *Discoveries*, ed. Lorna Hudson, in *The Cambridge Edition of the Works of Ben Jonson*, gen. eds. David Bevington, Martin Butler, and Ian Donaldson, 7 vols. (Cambridge: Cambridge University Press, 2012).

Jung, Sandro, "Illustrated Pocket Diaries and the Commodification of Culture," *Eighteenth-Century Life*, 37 (2013), 53–84.

Keates, Jonathan, *Handel: The Man and His Music*, rev. edn. (London: Bodley Head, 2008).

Kerrigan, John, "Shakespeare, Elegy, and Epitaph, 1557–1640," in Jonathan Post, ed., *The Oxford Handbook of Shakespeare's Poetry* (Oxford: Oxford University Press, 2013), 225–44.

Kewes, Paulina, "Shakespeare's Lives in Print, 1662–1821," in Robin Myers, Michael Harris, and Giles Mandelbrote, eds., *Lives in Print: Biography and the Book Trade from the Middle Ages to the 21st Century* (New Castle, DE: Oak Knoll Press, 2002), 55–82.

Kingsley-Smith, Jane, *The Afterlife of Shakespeare's Sonnets* (Cambridge: Cambridge University Press, 2019).

Kirwan, Peter, *Shakespeare and the Idea of Apocrypha: Negotiating the Boundaries of the Dramatic Canon* (Cambridge: Cambridge University Press, 2015).

Knight, Jeffrey Todd, *Bound to Read: Compilations, Collections, and the Making of Renaissance Literature* (Philadelphia: University of Pennsylvania Press, 2013).

Knight, Charles, *Passages of a Writing Life during Half a Century: with a Prelude of Early Reminiscences*, (London: Charles Knight & Co., 1873).

Kunin, Aaron, "Shakespeare's Preservation Fantasy," *PMLA*, 124 (January 2009), 92–106.

Langbaine, Gerard, *An Account of the English Dramatick Poets, or, Some observations and Remarks on the Lives and Writings of All Those That Have Publish'd Either Comedies, Tragedies, Tragi-comedies, Pastorals, Masques, Interludes, Farces or Opera's in the English Tongue* (1691).

Laoutaris, Chris, "The Prefatorial Material," in Emma Smith, ed., *The Cambridge Companion to Shakespeare's First Folio* (Cambridge: Cambridge University Press, 2016), 48–67.

Lee, Sidney, *A Life of William Shakespeare* (London: Smith, Elder & Co., 1898).

Lupić, Ivan, "Malone's Double Falsehood," in David Carnegie and Gary Taylor, eds., *The Quest for Cardenio: Shakespeare, Fletcher, Cervantes, and the Lost Play* (Oxford: Oxford University Press, 2012), 95–114.

MacKay, Ellen, "Acting Historical with Shakespeare, or, William-Henry Ireland's Oaken Chest," in Peter Holland, ed., *Shakespeare Survey* (Cambridge: Cambridge University Press, 2014), 202–20.

Malone, Edmond, *An Inquiry into the Authenticity of Certain Miscellaneous Papers and Legal Instruments Published [by S. W. H. Ireland], Dec. 24, 1795, and Attributed to Shakspeare, Queen Elizabeth, and Henry, Earl of Southampton ... Illustrated by Fac-similes of the Genuine Handwriting of That Nobleman, and of Her Majesty; A New Facsimile of the Handwriting of Shakspeare, and Other ... Documents, in a Letter, etc.* (1796).

Martin, Peter, *Edmond Malone, Shakespearean Scholar: A Literary Biography* (Cambridge: Cambridge University Press, 1995).

Mayer, Jean-Christophe, "Transmission as Appropriation: The Early Reception of John Benson's Edition of Shakespeare's Poems (1640)," *Journal of Early Modern Studies*, 5 (2016), 409–22.

McKitterick, David, *Old Books, New Technologies: The Representation, Conservation and Transformation of Books since 1700* (Cambridge: Cambridge University Press, 2013).

McMullan, Gordon, *Shakespeare and the Idea of Late Writing: Authorship in the Proximity of Death* (Cambridge: Cambridge University Press, 2007).

Meres, Francis, *Palladis Tamia. Wits Treasury, Being the Second Part of Wits Common Wealth* (1598).

Milton, John, *The Complete Works of John Milton, Vol. 3: The Shorter Poems*, ed. Barbara Kiefer Lewalski and Estelle Haan (Oxford: Oxford University Press, 2012).

Moseley, Humphrey, "The Stationer to the Reader," in *The Comedies and Tragedies Written by Francis Beaumont and Iohn Fletcher* (1647).

Murphy, Andrew, *Shakespeare in Print: A History and Chronology of Shakespeare Publishing* (Cambridge: Cambridge University Press, 2003).

Nashe, Thomas, "To the Gentlemen Students of Both Universities," preface to *Menaphon*, by Robert Greene (1589).

Newstok, Scott, *Quoting Death in Early Modern England: The Poetics of Epitaphs Beyond the Tomb* (Basingstoke: Palgrave Macmillan, 2009).

Orgel, Stephen, "Shakespeare and the Kinds of Drama," *Critical Inquiry*, 6 (Autumn 1979), 107–23.

Orgel, Stephen, "The Desire and Pursuit of the Whole," *Shakespeare Quarterly*, 58 (Fall 2007), 290–310.

Orlin, Lena Cowen, *The Private Life of William Shakespeare* (Oxford: Oxford University Press, 2021).

Ovid, *The. XV. Bookes of P. Ouidius Naso, Entytuled Metamorphosis*, trans. Arthur Golding (1567).

Ovid: *Metamorphoses*, trans. Frank Justus Miller (Cambridge, Mass.: Harvard University Press, 1951).

Pevsner, Nikolaus, and Alexandra Wedgwood, *Warwickshire: The Buildings of England* (London: Penguin Books, 1966).

Phillips, Edward, *Theatrum Poetarum, or, A Compleat Collection of the Poets* (1675).

Pope, Alexander, *The First Epistle of the Second Book of Horace, Imitated* (1737).

Priestley, Joseph, *A Chart of Biography* (1765).

Priestley, Joseph, *A Description of a Chart of Biography*, 4th edn. (1770).

Prior, James, *Life of Edmond Malone, Editor of Shakespeare* (London: Smith, Elder, & Co., 1860).

Quintilian, *The Orator's Education*, ed. and trans. Donald A. Russell, 5 vols. (Cambridge, MA: Harvard University Press, 2001).

Ramsey, Paul, *Fickle Glass: A Study of Shakespeare's Sonnets* (New York: AMS Press, 1979).

Reynolds, Joshua, *The Works of Sir Joshua Reynolds ... To which is Prefixed an Account of the Life and Writings of the Author by Edmond Malone* (London: T. Cadell, Jr. and W. Davies, 1801).

Roberts, David, *Thomas Betterton: The Greatest Actor of the Restoration Stage* (Cambridge: Cambridge University Press, 2010).

Roberts, Sasha, *Reading Shakespeare's Poems in Early Modern England* (New York: Palgrave Macmillan, 2003).

Rosenberg, Daniel, and Anthony Grafton, *Cartographies of Time* (New York: Princeton Architectural Press, 2010).

Rosenberg, Jessica, "The Point of the Couplet: Shakespeare's *Sonnets* and Tusser's *A Hundreth Good Pointes of Husbandrie*," *ELH*, 83 (2016), 1–41.

Rostenberg, Leona, "Thomas Thorpe: Publisher of 'Shakespeare's Sonnets,'" *The Papers of the Bibliographical Society of America*, 54 (First Quarter, 1960), 16–37.

Schlegel, August Wilhelm von, *A Course of Lectures on Dramatic Art and Literature*, trans. John Black, 2 vols. (London: Printed for Baldwin, Cradock, and Joy, 1815).

Schoch, Richard, *Writing the History of the British Stage: 1660–1900* (Cambridge: Cambridge University Press, 2016).

Schoenbaum, Samuel, *William Shakespeare: Records and Images* (London: Scolar Press, 1981).

Schoenbaum, Samuel, *Shakespeare's Lives*, new edn. (Oxford: Oxford University Press, 1991).

Scodel, Joshua, "Paradise Lost and Classical Ideals of Pleasurable Restraint," *Comparative Literature*, 48 (1996), 189–236.

Scott-Warren, Jason, "Commonplacing and Originality: Reading Francis Meres," *The Review of English Studies*, 68 (2017), 902–23.

Seneca, *The Seventh Tragedie of Seneca, Entitled Medea*, trans. John Studley (1566).

Seneca, *Hercules. Trojan Women. Phoenician Women. Medea. Phaedra*, ed. and trans. John G. Fitch (Cambridge, MA: Harvard University Press, 2002).

Shrank, Cathy, "Reading Shakespeare's Sonnets: John Benson and the 1640 Poems," *Shakespeare*, 5 (2009), 271–91.

Smith, Emma, *Shakespeare's First Folio: The Biography* (New York: Oxford University Press, 2016).

Smyth, Adam, *Autobiography in Early Modern England* (Cambridge: Cambridge University Press, 2010).

Stallybrass, Peter, "Editing as Cultural Formation: The Sexing of Shakespeare's Sonnets," in Marshall Brown, ed., *The Uses of Literary History* (Durham, NC: Duke University Press, 1995), 129–42.

Stallybrass, Peter, Roger Chartier, J. Franklin Mowery, and Heather Wolfe, "Hamlet's Tables and the Technologies of Writing in Renaissance England," *Shakespeare Quarterly*, 55 (Winter 2004), 379–419.

Stern, Tiffany, *Shakespeare, Malone and the Problems of Chronology* (Cambridge: Cambridge University Press, 2023).

Sweet, Rosemary, "Antiquaries and Antiquities in Eighteenth-Century England," *Eighteenth-Century Studies*, 34 (2001), 181–206.

Tate, Nahum, "Epistle Dedicatory," in *The History of King Lear: Acted at the Duke's Theatre* (1681).

Taylor, Gary, "Some Manuscripts of Shakespeare's Sonnets," *Bulletin of the John Rylands Library*, 68 (1985), 210–46.

Taylor, John, *Records of My Life* (London: Edward Bull, 1832).

van den Berg, Sarah, "Marking His Place: Ben Jonson's Punctuation," *Early Modern Literary Studies*, 1 (1995), 2.1–25.

Verstegen, Ian, "Death Dates, Birth Dates, and the Beginning of Art History," *Storiografia: Rivista annuale di storia*, 10 (2006), 1–19.

Vickers, Brian, ""Upstart Crow"? The Myth of Shakespeare's Plagiarism," *The Review of English Studies*, 68 (April 2017), 244–67.

Warton, Thomas, *The History of English Poetry, from the Close of the Eleventh to the Commencement of the Eighteenth Century*, 3 vols. (1781).

Winstanley, William, *The Lives of the Most Famous English Poets* (1686).

Wood, Anthony, *Athenæ Oxonienses. An Exact History of All the Writers and Bishops Who Have Had Their Education in the Most Ancient and Famous University of Oxford, from ... 1500 to the End of ... 1690 ...* (1691).

Wordsworth, William, "Essay, Supplementary to the Preface," in *Poems by William Wordsworth: Including Lyrical Ballads, and the Miscellaneous Pieces of the Author*, 2 vols. (London: Printed for Longman, Hurst, Rees, Orme, and Brown, 1815).

Woudhuysen, H. R., "Writing-Tables and Table-Books," *The Electronic British Library Journal* (2004), 3.1–11.

INDEX

Figures are indicated by an italic *f* following the page number.